Hand Weaving:

The Basics

Hand Weaving: The Basics

Lynn Gray Ross

B L O O M S B U R Y

LONDON · NEW DELHI · NEW YORK · SYDNEY

Bloomsbury Visual Arts
an imprint of Bloomsbury Publishing PLC
www.bloomsbury.com

Bloomsbury is a registered trade mark of Bloomsbury Publishing PLC

50 Bedford Square	1385 Broadway
London	New York
WC1B 3DP	NY 10018
UK	USA

© Lynn Gray Ross 2014

British Library cataloguing-in-publication data
A catalogue record for this book is available from the British Library

ISBN: PB: 978-1-4081-2899-2

Designed by Susan McIntyre
Illustrations on pages 32, 35, 53, 56, 58 and 64 by Alexa Rutherford
Printed and bound in China

Frontispiece photo: fenghui/Shutterstock.

Contents

To Blythe and Fern, with love from Grandma

Acknowledgements

I am most appreciative of my daughter Jill and my sons Chris and Simon for always being there when I need them. Their support in putting this book together and keeping production going while I wrestled with life-threatening illness has been invaluable, and their ironic sense of humour saw me through many tough moments.

My thanks go to all at Bloomsbury who have made it possible to produce this book, especially to Davida Forbes for her patience and understanding during the production process. Thanks are also due to Nigel Walker of Arran Photoco, to Alexa Rutherford for her wonderful artwork and to Sabrina Sangster for her plant drawings.

Astrid Hedberg taught me the basics of weaving on a small loom in the early 1970s in Stockholm as she helped me to adjust to being the mother of a small child in a new country surrounded by a new language. I am grateful for her care and attention and for my friendship over all these years with Astrid's daughter Kerstin, who keeps the weaving tradition alive in their family today.

The summer-school tutors at HV Skola in Stockholm in 1975, with their high standards and careful attention to detail, started me on a lifetime journey exploring weaving structures as a focus for my own creative development. Their pride in Swedish traditions sparked a curiosity about my own Scottish textile heritage, which in turn gave me the courage to move to Arran and set up my studio at Silverbirch. It was wonderful to visit them recently and to appreciate how much had come of a few summer weeks all those years ago.

There are so many other people who have been part of my weaving journey. Students, tutors and colleagues have all contributed their invaluable enthusiasm. Friends have been honest with their feedback over endless cups of coffee, and have picked up the pieces when all seemed to fall apart.

For all of this support I am extremely grateful.

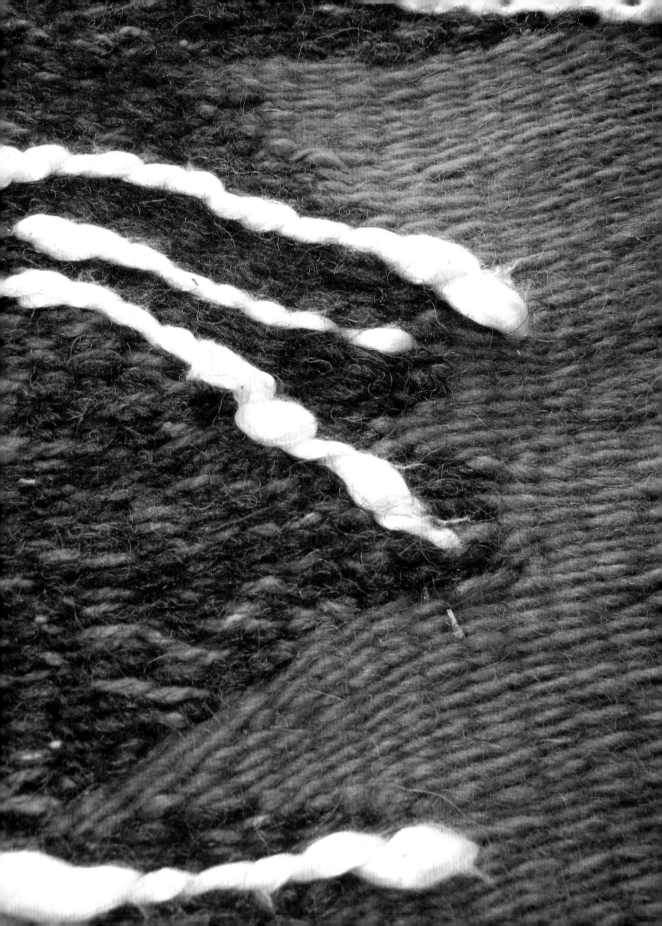

Foreword

This book is based on my 30 or so years of experience teaching weaving to adults and children. I began with classroom and curriculum work on the Isle of Arran, Scotland when my own children were small and I was asked to demonstrate weaving skills to primary pupils and explain their importance in the history of our island community.

Often I've witnessed my weaving students developing individual talents which otherwise might have remained hidden. One of my students with learning difficulties left school with no understanding or qualification in maths, even at a basic level. She could, however, calculate the most complicated weaves and understand the workings of a traditional loom with little tuition. What she couldn't conceive of theoretically was crystal clear when confronted with a practical weaving application.

Weaving is therapeutic. In a group situation tongues move as fast as fingers as the social aspects of practising a new skill enhance the whole experience. The additional satisfaction of a finished piece of weaving is a tangible reminder of time well spent. Frequently, adult learners attending my workshops express to me that after a lesson they feel satisfied and refreshed having spent time away from everyday problems, enjoying the new process and coming back to everyday concerns with a new perspective.

One poignant example of how weaving reaches farther than the craft itself centres around a shawl I wove in the studio at Silverbirch Spinning and Weaving Workshop in Arran. I used a fine Shetland hand-spun yarn produced on Arran in a basic plain weave with the occasional row of white hand-spun silk for contrast. I kept only sketchy records of my weaving in the early days and unfortunately never took a photograph of the shawl.

One of my students who helped with the shawl at the summer school at Silverbirch was a woman called Barbara from Toronto who was in remission from breast cancer. She loved her course and kept in touch for a few years, continuing to weave at home. I hung the finished shawl in the studio for three or four summers, puzzled as to why it didn't sell even though I tried different ways of displaying it.

OPPOSITE PAGE *Detail of* **After Iceland** *(2002), by the author. See page 80.*

One day, four women in their seventies came into the studio and introduced themselves as Barbara's mother and her sisters. Barbara had died the previous spring. Her mother and aunts had heard so much about the workshop and the time that Barbara spent there, that they came all the way from Poole in Dorset, UK to see the island and the studio. They were looking for a present for Barbara's daughter and went straight to the shawl, bought it and took it back with them to Dorset. A few weeks of weaving tuition for Barbara had results far beyond the craft itself.

The projects documented here have also been used to promote communication between generations in the classroom and in a community environment such as the local museum. The results provide many interesting anecdotes.

I hope that as you try out the suggestions in this book you will get a feeling for the craft and its possibilities, and that you will learn what does and doesn't suit you. There are times when you will feel utter frustration in following instructions and trying things out in practice. At this point you can go for a long walk and come back to the loom with a fresh perspective, and if that still doesn't work you can ask someone who knows to show you what to do.

This book is a collection of practical projects along with descriptions of work that I have done over the years. The patterns are straightforward enough for beginners to weave. They have been tried and tested in workshops with adults and children. I've also included background information on more complicated looms to encourage further exploration into this magical craft, again bearing in mind that learning to weave is a journey best undertaken with the help of an experienced teacher. I hope you will find the inspiration that I have found in weaving and in developing ideas with the confidence to try them out.

RIGHT *This illustration shows a weaver sitting in front of an Arabic upright loom, building up the design row by row. This type of loom is still used today to produce tapestries. Photo: Zurijeta/ Shutterstock.*

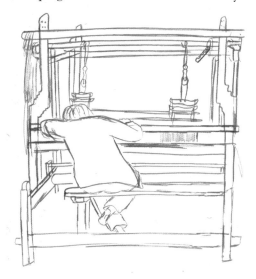

Lynn Didn't Get It, *a drawing of me by my friend, Inger Lindberg, when I attempted to teach myself a Finnish double weave. Learning to weave takes persistence!*

A brief history of weaving

Archaeological evidence shows that hand weaving has been a part of human life for thousands of years. Fragments of fine linen, woollen and silk cloth have been found in prehistoric grave sites in countries as far apart as China and Peru.

While most commercial weaving has been mechanised and is carried out in modern factories, traditional weaving practices have survived in many villages across the world. Separate areas are set aside for weaving where people work together to set up looms with enough yardage to meet the needs of several households or a whole community. These areas are a focus for social gatherings as people meet to discuss the affairs of the day, their hands occupied in creating the cloth.

Household goods created in this way are practical, made from fibres readily available in the immediate environment such as wool from sheep or alpacas, and plant fibres like flax, cotton and nettles. They are usually dyed with plant materials from the local area. Today such village weaving centres often produce cloth or rugs for the tourist market as well as for their own use.

OPPOSITE PAGE *Weaving at the Center for Traditional Textiles in Cuzco, Peru. This picture shows the threads being separated by a stick prior to the shuttle being woven across. Photo courtesy of Aracari Travel, Lima.*

FAR LEFT *Silk rug weaving on a hand loom in China, showing the threads arranged ready to weave. The pattern is developing on the loom row by row as the weaving progresses. Photo: Lee Prince/ Shutterstock.*

LEFT *This upright loom from Turkey shows how elaborate patterns could be developed using very basic equipment. The weaver sits in front of the loom, using hand-woven cushions for height and support. Photo: Connors Bros./ Shutterstock.*

Peruvian cloth samples. Photo courtesy of Aracari Travel, Lima.

These photos from Peru show a typical set-up for village weaving which can be found, for example, in Lesotho and other parts of Africa and in villages across Indonesia. Intricate designs can be created without the use of complex looms. Here the weavers use wooden sticks as simple aids.

ABOVE *Throughout history, the skill of weaving has been essential to the life of most communities. Weavers work together in Cuzco, Peru. Photo courtesy of Aracari Travel, Lima.*

LEFT *Setting up the loom at the Center for Traditional Textiles in Cuzco. In good weather, hand weaving is carried on outdoors with portable equipment. Photo courtesy of Aracari Travel, Lima.*

RIGHT *Setting up the warp at Cuzco. Photo courtesy of Aracari Travel, Lima.*

BELOW *Community weaving at the Center for Traditional Textiles in Cuzco, Peru, to produce textiles for sale. Photo courtesy of Aracari Travel, Lima.*

Looms: a brief introduction

The craft of weaving has developed over the centuries in two distinct directions: (1) lengths of cloth and (2) tapestry pictures and rugs. Both are produced on a piece of specially constructed equipment known as a loom. The purpose of any loom is to hold one set of threads (the warp) under tension to make it possible to weave another set of threads (the weft). The result is known as the web or cloth. Looms come in a variety of shapes and sizes with different mechanical systems, but their basic function is the same. They are used worldwide in making rugs and cloths for decorative effects, often producing complicated-looking results from simple techniques.

EARLY UPRIGHT LOOMS

Early looms were generally simple constructions which could be easily dismantled and re-assembled to suit a nomadic lifestyle. They were made from twigs, branches and other found objects, like stones or clay weights which were tied to the end of the warp threads to control weight and tension. The threads were often attached to a tree or boat mast to provide tension and mobility. As people became more settled, and looms became a fixture in early houses, these looms were modified to allow the weaver to produce patterns in the cloth, until the Industrial Revolution when looms were mechanised and moved into factories.

LEFT *This basic loom from Greece shows how the warp threads are held in tension by tree branches so that the weft threads can be woven across to form the web or weave.*

Drawing of a Gobelin tapestry loom, published in Magasin Pittoresque, *Paris, 1845. Photo: Antonio Abrigani/Shutterstock.*

Each loom in this photo from Cuzco, Peru is attached to the wooden log at the top to provide tension. Photo courtesy of Aracari Travel, Lima.

This loom is used to produce lengths of cloth. The picture shows how the weft threads are separated by a system of strings and pulleys, raised and lowered with the foot pedals to create alternative sheds. Photo: Patrick Foto/ Shutterstock.

A row of textile looms weaving cotton yarn in a textile mill. Photo: Rehan Qureshi/Shutterstock.

FRAME LOOMS

Frame looms are ideal for creating a finished piece of fixed dimensions, and are most often used for rugs, cushion covers or tapestries. This book will concentrate on the use of the frame loom to practise small projects and try out elaborate techniques for use on a larger scale. This introduction will give you an idea of how looms have developed over the centuries and help you determine where your own interests might lie.

Large frame loom showing a half-woven rug. Photo: liubomir/Shutterstock

Hand weaving in the twenty-first century

The development of weaving and looms up to the twenty-first century varies worldwide. Industrialisation in some European countries and in the USA meant that cottage weaving became redundant in the late eighteenth century. In other areas of the world, such as Peru, village production has changed very little and old techniques and practices are used in contemporary settings.

Nowadays practical hand weaving is carried out for more reasons than simple household need. Industrialisation in western society has made it unnecessary and uneconomical to produce textiles by hand. In recent

Cloth produced at Cuzco, Peru. Photograph courtesy of Aracari Travel, Lima.

decades the UK's textile industry has deteriorated and in some cases disappeared entirely. We have exported our machinery, skills and expertise, which we developed during the Industrial Revolution and beyond, to the rapidly expanding factories in countries where labour is relatively cheap and production costs allow for competitive marketing on a global scale.

Until the nineteenth century in western society, hand weavers were respected for their skills. They were often wealthy and in demand for their essential and decorative work. The skills of hand weaving are now handed on more for their craft and artistic value than out of any sense of necessity. Hand weaving is still a vital part of the economy in developing countries both in terms of preserving traditions and attracting tourists to see first-hand how traditional textiles are produced.

BELOW *Belt from Cuzco, Peru (c. 2010), 120 x 4 cm. Purchased from makers at the local produce market. This woven belt shows how an intricate pattern can be woven on a simple loom. The pattern is formed by lifting in sequence threads which are in held in tension by the loom. These patterns and their production method date back to antiquity. Photo courtesy of Aracari Travel, Lima.*

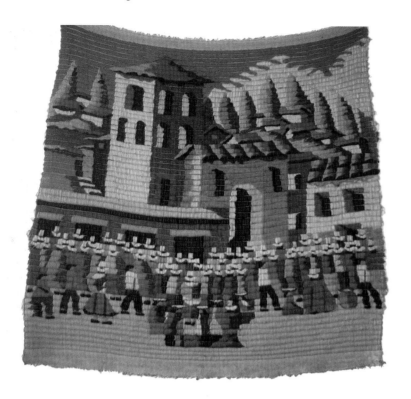

LEFT *Weaving from a village market near Ambato in Ecuador, 2009. 92 x 92 cm. The weaving is worked in unspun carded wool, space-dyed to create the colour arrangements which form the completed picture. This work provides an example of contemporary techniques illustrating the type of architecture in the village, while giving a glimpse of village life.*

ABOVE *Belts from Guatemala and Mexico. Top: cotton, 10 x 184 cm; centre: wool, 2 x 92 cm; bottom: cotton, 9 x 130 cm. These belts echo the designs which are produced worldwide in cotton and wool on simple looms, primarily for the tourist trade. Purchased in the marketplace in Guanajuato, Mexico in 1968.*

Projects such as the Center for Traditional Textiles in Cuzco, Peru are being encouraged by local and national governments and international agencies. Examples from this project in Peru and photos of belts from Mexico and Guatemala, as well as the stunning depiction of a Guatemalan village, demonstrate the type of weaving that is produced nowadays primarily for the tourist trade.

In the late 1970s I took part in such a programme as a consultant for the government of Lesotho. They were beginning to explore possibilities for developing traditional crafts as part of the village economy. I was asked to test hand-spun samples of mohair with the traditional dyes we had reintroduced in the workshop on Arran such as indigo and madder, because their traditions were in danger of being lost. The original aim was to market the dyed yarns. Village projects in Lesotho have flourished, and a factory-based weaving industry has developed, providing employment and education for women.

Other community projects are regulated by fair-trade organisations such as Traidcraft (www.traidcraft.co.uk) and also run by co-operatives to ensure that as much of the income as possible from the sale of woven goods goes back into the community to meet basic needs. Production is done by traditional methods, adapting designs to the needs of modern market prices.

There is also a new awareness of the need to control exploitation of weavers, especially addressing the problem of child labour, ensuring that health and safety are paramount and that children are provided with a basic education as part of their working day.

In the western world we can afford to import textile goods produced in developing countries. Unfortunately this means that we have lost contact with textile production as part of our daily lives. We have lost contact too with the master weavers who practise the skills. Along with the loss of practical knowledge and skills, we have lost the opportunity that hand textile production provided to bring people together to socialise and pass on techniques to the next generation.

Many societies have a rich history of mythology, stories and music based on textiles; weaving has often been considered a sacred occupation and tales are told of the magical properties of looms and spinning wheels. In many cultures, for example the Navajo in south-western USA, weaving is directly linked to mythology and to beliefs about how the world was created. In the process of acquiring the techniques of this ancient craft, learners of all ages connect to their own culture and heritage, at the same time exploring their own capabilities.

Official bodies like the United Nations and the European Union have recognised that traditional crafts have economic potential in improving village life, especially when they are presented as part of a tourism package. There is now also consideration in official programmes for 'responsible sourcing', i.e. prioritising environmental issues in the choice of raw materials and production methods. Development is robust, in spite of the changes in society. It is more important to celebrate and grow the traditions which have survived and to share knowledge and expertise wherever we can.

Arran Flowering Cherry, by the author (1976). 50 x 50 cm. Woven with hand-dyed mohair samples from Lesotho and natural sheep's wool.

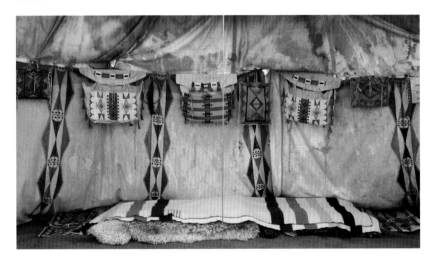

Interior of a Navajo tent showing traditional weaving. Photo: MarFot/Shutterstock.

Types of weaving

Cloth-weaving

Cloth-weaving involves lifting up selected warp threads to form a gap through which the weft is passed. This gap is called the shed. The craft of weaving cloth is based on mathematics. Look closely and you will discover an inbuilt design in the fabric, calculated during the setting-up process to repeat itself along the width and length of the fabric. The counting system used to set up a loom can be used to devise lifting sequences which create elaborate patterns. Learning to control the setting-up of the loom leads to endless design possibilities and colour arrangements.

One traditional silk-weaving loom from China has perhaps the most unusual mechanism for lifting the weft threads and forming the shed. In addition to the weaver, another very agile man sits on top of the loom and manipulates the pattern threads to be lifted in the next row. This threading has to be accurate, in order for the pattern to weave correctly. Not surprisingly, the life of the man who 'programmed' the loom was well insured, not only for the physical risk but also for his knowledge of intricate patterns.

LEFT *On this loom the warp is threaded in a sequence of four threads through vertical strings which are known as heddles. The heddles are then lifted to form the shed so that two threads are up and two down. The pattern in the weave is formed by manipulating which warp threads are up and which are down. Photo: Photogrape/ Shutterstock.*

OPPOSITE PAGE *Photo: stefanodinenno/Shutterstock.*

LEFT *Cloth woven at Silverbirch Workshop on the Isle of Arran c. 1980. Below: hand-spun tartan, dyed with cochineal. Top: striped wool cloth based on traditional 'drugget' skirt material from the island.*

BELOW *Swedish 4-shaft loom showing warp threads in preparation for threading through the string heddles, which are distributed evenly over the four sets of sticks. This allows for more complicated patterns to be woven than on the frame loom where there are only two openings.*

ABOVE *Built just before looms were mechanised and moved into factories, this nineteenth-century wooden loom performs the same function as the simple frame, with the additional possibility of winding the warp thread round the back and front beams to create longer lengths of cloth. There is also a system of lifting threads by using foot treadles to create patterns.*

RIGHT *This photo shows warp threads divided into six separate groups, known as shafts. These allow more complicated patterns to be woven, compared to the simple frame loom. Photo: Richard Peterson/Shutterstock.*

Examples of 'overshot' cloth-weaving in the patterns Damsel Arise *and* John Madison *by members of the Spinning and Weaving Guild in Detroit, Michigan, c. 1980, 44 x 48 cm.*

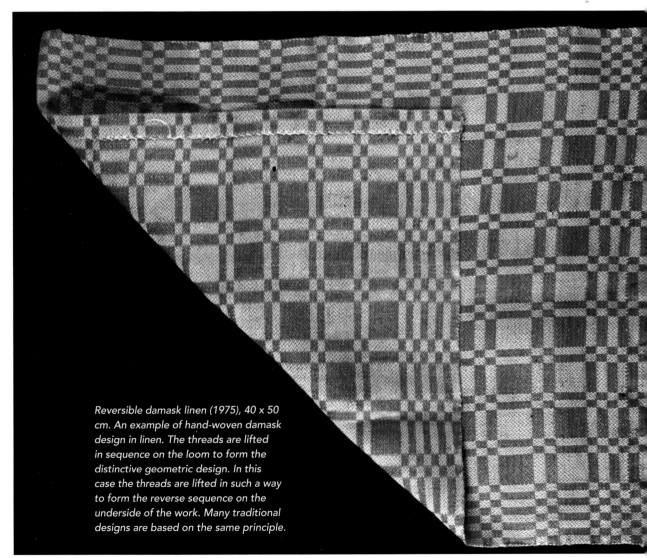

Reversible damask linen (1975), 40 x 50 cm. An example of hand-woven damask design in linen. The threads are lifted in sequence on the loom to form the distinctive geometric design. In this case the threads are lifted in such a way to form the reverse sequence on the underside of the work. Many traditional designs are based on the same principle.

Tapestry-weaving

There is confusion sometimes as 'tapestry' also refers to embroidery or cross stitch, which are worked with a needle on a cloth background. In weaving when we refer to tapestry we are talking about pictures or geometric designs created row by row on a plain coloured thread which is usually hidden as the surface picture grows. What makes tapestry-weaving endlessly fascinating is that the design is woven horizontally to give a final vertical effect. The skill is to learn how to develop curves and diagonals on the surface of the weave while creating a sturdy fabric without gaps.

On the whole, tapestry-weaving is more of a decorative pursuit than cloth-weaving, with the aim of producing wall-hangings and other works of art, though smaller items such as purses, rugs and cushion covers are examples of practical applications of this ancient technique. Historically, however, large tapestries provided both decoration and insulation in desert tents and draughty European castles.

Detail of a medieval-style tapestry, showing a woman playing a psaltery with a quill. Photo: Durden Images/Shutterstock

Woven tapestries have been found dating back to at least the third century BC. In the early fourteenth century the craft was developed in Germany and Switzerland, expanding over time to France and the Netherlands. In the fourteenth and fifteenth centuries, tapestries were produced in professional workshops, and by the sixteenth century Flanders had become the centre of European tapestry production. Many examples of this work have been preserved in museums and stately homes. These large tapestries were woven on a grand scale, with a team of weavers working on each one. Sometimes the designs were woven using a drawing on paper as a guide. These drawings were known as cartoons; they were attached to the loom in front of the tapestry, while the weavers worked from the back, using the cartoon to develop the intricate detail of pattern and colour.

Kilims from the Middle East and Navajo weavings from the south-western United States are traditional examples of tapestry-weaving, using designs that have been used for centuries. The basic tools have remained much the same since the early tapestries were woven.

A pattern of geometric animals and birds in a traditional Turkish kilim. Photo: Steve Estvanik/ Shutterstock.

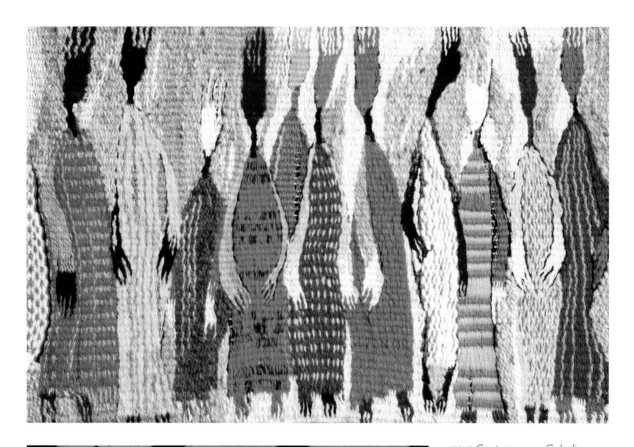

ABOVE *Contemporary Gobelin-style tapestry from Africa. The figures in this weaving have been woven from side to side across the width of the loom. When the weaving is cut from the loom the side edges form the top and bottom of the weave. Using this technique reduces the number of threads that have to be interwoven across the row to form the long, slim figures. Photo: Helena-Ogorodnikova/Shutterstock.*

LEFT *Detail of contemporary tapestry from Ecuador. Photo: Katarzyna Citko/Shutterstock.*

Birthday Balloons *(1986), wool and cotton, by the author. 90 x 120 cm. This tapestry was woven to celebrate my son Chris' tenth birthday party and shows the moment when a roomful of boys burst outside to chase balloons. The background was woven with simple plain weave in hand-dyed wool to echo the surrounding fields and sky. The figures were woven by lifting a few threads and wrapping cotton yarn around to form the shapes. The idea was inspired by a little box of Guatemalan worry dolls, which are small figures formed by wrapping yarn round tiny sticks. The idea is to put the dolls underneath your pillow and let them do the worrying for you. Not so sure about the ten-year-old boys!*

Tapestries are still produced in studios across Europe and in other parts of the world where medieval techniques are given a contemporary interpretation.

The process
of weaving

Weaving is a series of steps, each involving skills and techniques, that must be completed as accurately as possible as a basis for the next step. The journey of weaving involves taking each step of the process as it comes, completing it with patience so that the techniques are as accurate as possible.

Following the weaving process is never about speed or material gain; it is more about how the weaver develops along with the cloth, often in unexpected ways. It can be frustrating in the beginning, as with any new skill, but perseverance brings its own rewards. By starting with simple looms and designs, experience eventually brings a sense of control and understanding.

The frame loom

As a beginner, it is best to choose the simplest loom to warp up and practise weaving, which is a small frame loom. A frame loom is a frame with evenly spaced grooves across the top and bottom, and is an excellent tool to begin to explore the craft of weaving. They are available in a variety of sizes to suit the weaver and the project. Patterns are simple, and this provides the teacher or the learner with an endless supply of ideas and projects to build on, encouraging short and long-term interest in the craft and related subjects. Working with simple techniques on a frame loom produces a finished piece quite quickly, which gives an immediate sense of accomplishment.

The frame loom has the advantage of being portable and quick to assemble. Fruit crates or other sturdy boxes can be used to fashion a frame loom if ready-made looms are not conveniently available or wood for construction is scarce. Small nails or tacks can be spaced evenly at the top and bottom of the loom if the wood is not strong enough to have grooves cut into it. The most important thing is that the frame is stable so that the warp can be threaded up with firm tension. The frame should also hold its rectangular shape as pressure builds up as the weaving progresses.

The size of a frame loom allows for an appropriate weave to be set up for a short afternoon workshop, or a piece that can be developed over a week or even several weeks, depending on the spacing of the warp threads.

OPPOSITE PAGE *Large frame loom showing a half-woven rug. Photo: liubomir/Shutterstock.*

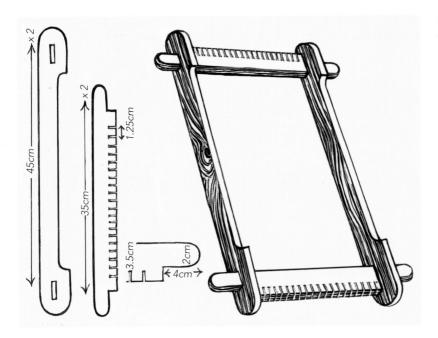

Template for building a small frame loom.

BUILDING A FRAME LOOM

The template above shows how to construct a small rectangular weaving frame. The proportions are based on a traditional tapestry loom which keeps warp threads evenly spaced and provides essential tension. The dimensions can be expanded to make a larger frame with the same proportions of width and length. The diagram shows the shapes needed for each piece that will ensure the loom fits together to form a rigid frame.

FRAME SIZE

For beginners, a frame of approximately 45 x 35 cm (18 x 14 inches) is the most suitable. I've tried many different versions of frame looms, but find the most useful to be those with grooves cut along the top and bottom bar, preferably 4 grooves per 2.5 cm (1 inch). This size frame will therefore have around 56 grooves along the top and bottom bars.

This size of loom is a good width for beginners to learn the basic techniques of changing colours and weaving stripes. It also allows the first piece to be finished quite quickly, which is satisfying and helps to build confidence. A smaller loom may be used by more experienced weavers to practise how to lift the threads in sequence to form more complicated patterns or to try out design and colour before committing to a more ambitious work.

Bear in mind the finished piece doesn't have to be limited by the dimensions that you can produce on the frame loom. You can weave several shapes and strips in the same basic colour and design and mount them together to form a larger piece. This inspirational idea is illustrated here by a piece of traditional indigo-dyed Kente cloth from Kenya. It can also be incorporated into a contemporary design such as *Galway Hooker* on pages 46–7.

After trying out some ideas on the small frame loom, you may want to progress to a larger version of the frame loom, ideally 50 x 80 cm (20 x 32 inches) with the same groove spacing. The larger frame is suitable for older children (depending on height) and for adults.

The procedure for setting up warp threads on a frame loom is the same regardless of the size of the frame.

Shuttles

Shuttles are tools around which weft yarns are wound to keep them in order and carry them across the shed, the opening which is formed when the warp threads are separated. Small versions of the shuttles which are used on large floor looms, shown in the picture below left, are an excellent way to keep yarn in order. These shuttles in the image below are an appropriate size for the frame loom projects in this book: 12.5 cm (5 inches) for the small loom and 25 cm (10 inches) for the larger frame loom and the tapestry frame, all of them 2.5 cm (1 inch) wide.

You can wind yarn around the shuttle to a thickness which will fit through the shed you form with your hands or with the mechanics of the loom, such as foot pedals.

More sophisticated shuttles are used in mechanically operated looms that are often programmed to weave without the aid of a weaver's hands. These can move with great speed and are often known as 'flying shuttles'.

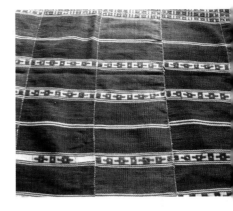

Kente cloth. Strips of weaving are sewn together to form a wider piece of cloth which is eventually made into a simple garment. This technique has been used worldwide where looms are narrow but wider cloth is required for clothing or other practical use.

BELOW LEFT *Shuttles ready for weaving.*

BELOW RIGHT *A traditional boat shuttle, so called because of its shape. Used for holding fine yarn which is wound around the central bobbin, these were later mechanised to go through the shed at high speed. Photo: Pavelgr/ Shutterstock.*

Choosing thread thickness and colour

The key to weaving is the relationship between warp and weft. If you space your threads every inch instead of every ½ inch, the weft would cover the warp threads, giving what we call a weft face weave, where the warp is hidden, apart from the top and bottom fringes on the loom. This also happens if you use a finer warp thread than weft.

If, on the other hand, you warp up with a thicker thread and use a finer thread for your weft, the warp threads will be drawn together into a vertical design. This is used to form the patterns in traditional belts or ribbons. This is a warp face weave.

The choice of colour vertically and horizontally will influence the look of the finished weaving, as much as the balance between vertical and horizontal threads. The best way to find out how colours work in weaving is to experiment. Build up your own portfolio of ideas and see what works for you. When you are learning, keep it simple and choose colours that you like to work with.

In this sample the warp threads are green, pink and red, and the weft threads are red and blue. This close-up also shows how thickness of weft relates to warp spacing. Photo: BrankaVV/Shutterstock.

Starting to weave

Choose a weft thread that will cover the warp as you weave. Fill the shuttle by winding the thread around until you have enough yarn to finish a few rows of continuous weaving. Wind just enough so that the shuttle will fit between the rows when one row is lifted above the other.

WARPING UP

Keeping the correct tension in the warp and weft is the key to successful weaving. It's something that comes with practice and not force: experience will gradually give you confidence in judging the overall tension.

If you are starting your first ever weave, begin by warping up 12 threads. This is a good number to get the feel of how the weave works. Later you can add threads to make the weaving wider. Mark the centre of the top bar of the loom with a felt tip pen or pencil. Count six grooves to the left of centre of the loom and tie the yarn firmly round that groove. Use the weaver's knot as illustrated opposite. This will provide a firm base for controlling the tension as you wind the warp on to the rest of the loom.

Once you've tied the initial knot, stretch the thread gently round the opposite groove at the bottom of the loom, making sure that the thread is firm but still has some elasticity.

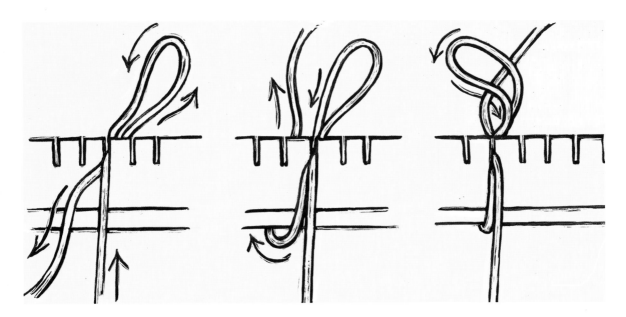

Bring the yarn back up to the top of the loom and gently hook it round the next groove, then back down and around the next groove on the bottom bar. Check with your hand that the two warp lengths are about the same tension.

Continue to feed the warp from the top to the bottom bar and back until you have 12 threads, making sure that each new warp thread is the same tension as the others. This is especially important when you warp on the last string. Tie the yarn firmly to the top on the 12th groove using the same weaver's knot and the loom is ready to weave. Don't forget to check the tension before you tie the knot and make sure the knot doesn't slip as it falls into place.

The warping-up procedures given for the projects in this book should give you a starting point to create your own weavings and gradually give you the knowledge required to vary the basic instructions to achieve your own effects. Just remember that the main aim is to provide an even tension in the threads across the width of the warp so that weaving is straightforward and the result is as neat as possible.

ABOVE *How to tie a weaver's knot.*

BELOW *A frame with 12 warp threads*

COMFORT AT THE FRAME LOOM

It is important to arrange your working space so that the frame sits comfortably in your lap, resting at an angle against a table so there is no strain on the arms or wrists. Experiment with different sizes and spacings until you find one that you are most relaxed with.

It is also crucial to use a chair that prevents neck and shoulder strain and keeps the head and chin at a comfortable angle. Taking frequent breaks to stretch the body, especially the arms, neck and shoulders, will help to keep the body supple.

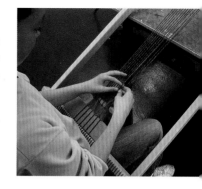

Arrange your working space so that the loom rests in your lap at an angle that is comfortable for you.

FIRST STEPS IN PLAIN WEAVE

When you are starting to weave it is best to choose a simple pattern such as plain weave, where the technique of lifting alternate threads in each row is easy to manipulate with the hands. To begin, weave a few strips of cardboard 2.5 cm (1 inch) into the warp threads. These will help to hold the warp threads in place and prevent the sides of the weaving from sloping in to form a 'lighthouse' shape, which is only desirable if you're weaving a lighthouse.

Go over the first thread, under the second and so on to the end of the row. Follow the opposite sequence – under the first thread, over the second – for the next row. It is important to establish the weaving sequence carefully in the first few rows so that you can see how the pattern develops and check that there are no mistakes at the beginning. After a few rows it becomes easier to see which thread goes over and which under. You can see in the photo below of the cardboard strips that the top strip went over the first warp thread on the loom and then under the second, over the third, under the fourth and so on to the end of the row.

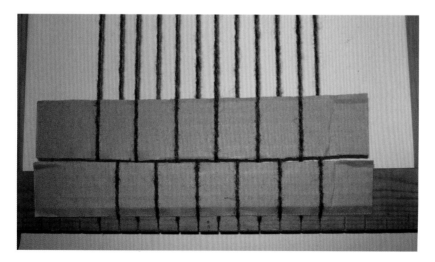

WEAVING THE FIRST WEFT THREAD

A medium-weight yarn such as Aran thickness or cotton rug yarn will work best to give you an idea of how weaving works. Taking the shuttle loaded with your weft thread, follow the opposite sequence used for the previous cardboard strip. Use your fingers to lift the threads that you should go under in the next row. This helps you to see which way to go. When you get to the end of the row, pull the yarn through and leave a 7 cm (3 inch) tail at the beginning of the row. Weave this tail over the first two threads and tuck it behind.

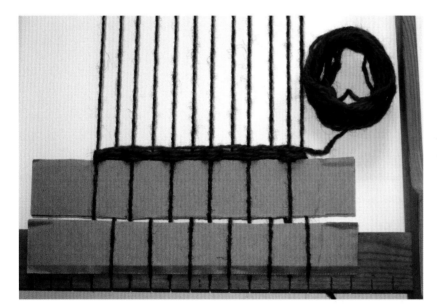

LEFT *After three rows you can begin to see the fabric or web forming on the loom.*

BELOW *As you weave, there is a cumulative tendency for the sides to pull in. You can prevent this by gently beating the warp down across the row, either with your fingers or with a shuttle, leaving a small loop to form a gap at the side of each row. This gap will disappear as the pressure from the following rows takes hold and will keep the edges straight.*

CONTROLLING WEFT TENSION

Now you're ready to come back across with the shuttle, making sure that you change the sequence and go over the threads you went under last time and under the threads you went over. If you concentrate on weaving across the rows and don't pull the weft thread tight, you will gradually get a feeling of how to keep the edges straight.

Keep going and practise this tension control. You will gradually understand how it should be and will eventually be able to get it right without thinking about it. If anyone points out your uneven edges when you're learning, just tell them it is a deliberate feature in your design, and keep on practising!

FORMING THE SHED

When the warp threads are separated across the row, they form an opening called the shed. In the beginning it is best to choose a simple pattern such as plain weave, where the technique of lifting alternate threads in each row is easy to manipulate with the hands. For example, on the first row in the sample warp of 12 threads just described, lift every other thread with your hand so that you have 6 threads pulled up to leave the opening for the shed. On the second row, lift the other six threads across the loom so that the threads which were lifted in row 1 are now underneath and the alternate 6 threads are pulled up to form the shed.

The basic process is to weave the weft thread across the shed to form the weave, the most simple being this two-row repeating pattern called plain weave. You can try out these techniques on the small frame loom to give you an idea of how they work in practice.

The shed can be formed by hand, by the use of foot pedals or by an elaborately programmed computerised loom. The illustrations show how the shed is formed in different types of looms.

LEFT *A stick shuttle passes through alternate threads to form the shed. The weft thread is woven across the shed to begin the weave. Photo: RonGreer.Com/ Shutterstock.*

TOP AND BOTTOM RIGHT *Hands forming the shed ready for the weft. This technique can be used effectively on the small frame-weaving projects in this book. Photo: Mikhail Olykainen/ Shutterstock.*

The shed open ready for the weft to be woven across. Photo: Yuyangc/Shutterstock.

Traditional Indonesian loom-stick holding the shed open so that the weaver is free to weave a pattern across the work. Photo: gualtiero boffi/Shutterstock.

This is the basic principle used to form the weave, regardless of the type of loom used. Repeating this alternating lifting sequence will gradually build up the fabric to the desired length. This length is limited only by the size and type of loom used. Experience will tell you what suits you best and what you most like to weave.

ADDING TO THE WEFT THREAD OR INTRODUCING A NEW COLOUR

Weave at least 12 rows to get a feeling of how the weaving will look, before you change colours. You can make each colour as wide as you like. Finish the weft thread or first colour at the end of a row by cutting the yarn, leaving a length of yarn or tail. Weave this tail round the end warp thread, over warp threads 2 and 3 and push it through to the back of the work to be trimmed when the weaving is finished.

Next row: starting on the other side of the loom, weave the new colour across the row, leaving a length of yarn or tail. Go back and weave the tail round the end warp thread, under warp threads 2 and 3 and over thread 4, through to the back to be trimmed later.

Finish the second colour at the end of a row, weave in the tail as described above and start the first colour again on the other side. Continue this way until the weaving is complete.

FINISHING OFF THE WEAVING

1. Leave 12.5–15 cm (5–6 inches) of warp thread above the top of the weaving to make a fringe when the weaving is cut off the loom.

2. Turn the loom so the cardboard strips are at the top, with the wrong side of the work facing you. The bottom of the weave is now at the top.

3. Trim off the tails where you've changed colours or added new weft threads, leaving about ¼ inch of yarn.

4. Carefully cut across the threads, which are now at the bottom edge of the loom (the top edge should still be held by the frame).

5. Taking three warp threads at a time, tie them in a knot at the bottom edge of the weaving to stop the work from unravelling. You should have 4 knots along the bottom edge if you started with 12 threads on the loom.

6. Now gently pull out the cardboard strips and unhook the loops from the grooves at the top of the loom.

7. Take a length of wood or driftwood a few inches wider than the weaving and thread it through the loops.

8. Untie the knots on either end of the top and form two more loops the same length as the others, then darn the end of the remaining yarn invisibly along the edge of the weaving for 5 cm (2 inches) anchoring with a backstitch.

9. Twist or braid a length of yarns and loop this over the two ends of the wood or driftwood to make a wall-hanging.

OPPOSITE PAGE

TOP LEFT *Weaving ready to finish off either as a wall-hanging or a purse.*

TOP RIGHT *Loom is turned around so the bottom of the weave becomes the top. The new bottom threads are cut off the loom.*

BOTTOM LEFT *Weaving ready for driftwood.*

BOTTOM RIGHT *Finished wall-hanging.*

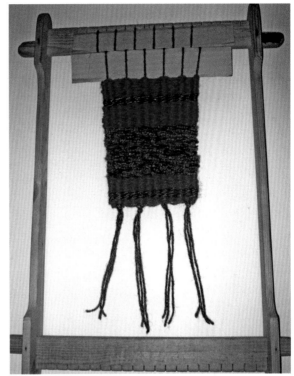

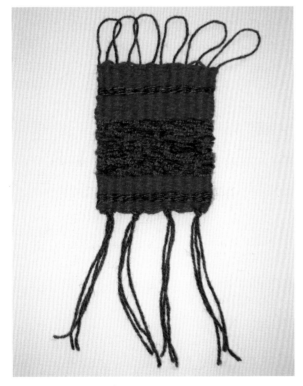

Project: small purse

YOU WILL NEED

- small frame loom
- sharp scissors
- darning needle with a large eye
- button
- for the weft, a selection of bright-coloured yarns, at least Aran thickness, or finer yarns woven as one to form thicker yarn.

TO MAKE THE PURSE

1. Set up the loom as for the wall-hanging on page 41 and follow the weaving instructions until you have 7.5–10 cm (3–4 inches) of warp left at the top.

2. Cut the top and bottom warp threads and remove the cardboard strips.

3. Thread each warp thread invisibly down through the weave for at least 5 cm (2 inches). Trim edges.

4. Fold the weaving in three so that the middle part forms the back of the purse. Using a darning needle sew the edges of the back and middle sections of the purse together, following the edge of the weaving.

5. Using two lengths of thread, form a loop at the middle of the top flap. Sew the two lengths together.

6. Sew a button on to the bottom flap. Fold the flap over and button the two parts together to close the purse.

Purse with button fastening.

Back of purse.

Project: tartan sample

This sample is a tartan woven in plain weave. Samples are useful for practice and to test colour combinations to add to your portfolio.

The word 'tartan' has its origin in the French word *tartaine*, meaning 'speckled' in the manner of a hen or a trout. It is a very old design which made use of local fibres and plants. The dye plants available varied in different regions, which led to the idea of family tartans. Tartan was very practical because the weaver was able to use up smaller quantities of yarn from earlier projects, or small dye lots from plants that were not plentiful.

YOU WILL NEED

- small frame loom

  2-ply thick hand-spun yarn or equivalent in at least two colours

The yarns pictured here are dyed with plants, madder and indigo. By using the same thickness of yarn in the weft thread, a balance is created in the weave, so the dark blue in the centre of the sequence should be more or less square. Knot the colours as you change them at the end of the loom as shown right, so that they can't slip.

For the warp, over 20 threads (10 each side of the centre of the loom), I've followed the sequence:

- 2 threads pale blue
- 4 threads madder orange
- 8 threads darker blue
- 4 threads madder orange
- 2 threads pale blue

When the loom is warped up, weave in two rows of cardboard strips (2.5 cm or 1 inch wide) so that there will be enough warp threads to form a fringe when the weave is cut off the loom.

Now weave the weft, following the same colour sequence:

- 2 rows pale blue
- 4 rows madder orange
- 8 rows dark blue
- 4 rows madder orange
- 2 rows pale blue

Keep a light hand and you will gradually learn to control the tension to produce the fabric and look that you would like as a result.

To finish the piece, unhook the yarn loops from the grooves on the loom and cut the loops across the centre to form two threads. Lay the weaving flat and knot the two threads together across the width of the top and bottom to keep the sample from unravelling.

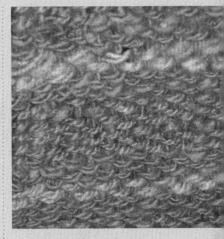

Plain-weave tartan sample.

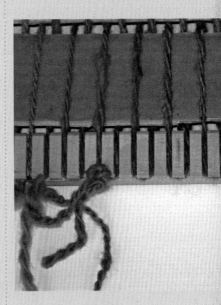

Knot the colours as you change them so that they can't slip.

43

Larger tapestry looms

The tension screws on top of the loom can be tightened to help keep the weave in place as it grows. Wood is used instead of cardboard to help keep the initial few rows in tension across the width of the loom. The weaving is part of a project for the 1995 United Nations Conference on Women in Beijing, which is described on pages 100–101. This loom produces work up to 1 x 1 m (39 x 39 inches).

The large tapestry looms are an investment and again some experience with the small frame will help you decide if this is something you want to pursue.

ABOVE *Large tapestry frame with* **Arran** *weaving (see pages 100–101 for more about this tapestry). This loom was built on Arran in the 1980s on the same principle as the smaller frames, with supporting 'legs' on the back to provide stability.*

LEFT *A vintage wooden loom. Photo: Arogant/Shutterstock.*

Found-object looms

Larger pieces can also be woven which combine small strips of weave with found objects such as driftwood or shells with holes created by nature. As I live on an island, my reference point for found-object looms is generally what turns up on the beach – curved driftwood, old lobster traps, wood from old boats with rusty nails, can all be pressed into service as found-object looms.

RIGHT *Weavelet by author. 6 x 15 cm. Another source of raw material for a loom is a hoop made of willow or any other supple wood to form a circular base for a 'weavelet' or strip of inspired colour. This one is based on a larger piece called* **Celtic Wedding**, *and uses unspun white silk and linen and cochineal-dyed red wool. A braid or cord attached for hanging creates a harmonious whole, using the yarns which are in the weaving.*

LEFT **Lobster Pot** *(2006). 45 x 5 cm. Hand-spun natural dyed wool and unspun white silk weaving. The crosspieces from an old lobster pot made an ideal loom, especially since there were rusty nails still attached to hold the warp threads.*

ABOVE **Spindrift** *(2002). Hand-spun weaving on driftwood loom made with grey Shetland handspun wool and white silk. Usually the form of the found object provides inspiration for the design of the weaving, as in this marvellous piece of driftwood. The finished result, with a braid or cord attached for hanging, creates a harmonious whole. The possibilities are endless; there is no such thing as a mistake when creating these one-off pieces.*

Project for a larger frame loom: a wall hanging

Found objects can be the inspiration for an entire piece, as with this shell with a hole, which provided the colourway for the *Galway Hooker* weaving, pictured right. The piece was woven on a frame loom. The driftwood used to hang the finished piece provides added interest with its sea creature eye etched by sea and sand to expose the grain.

Galway Hooker is inspired by the characteristic red-sailed boats which were found in Galway Bay and many other fishing communities in the British Isles and other Atlantic countries. The weaving was produced on a large frame loom, showing again how the finished width of the wall-hanging is not limited by the width of the loom.

Texture is created by the use of two different yarns dyed in the same natural indigo vat. One is 2-ply Shetland softspun and the other is from a beginner at hand spinning with that unique uneven texture which is difficult to duplicate once you become proficient at spinning (cherish those first efforts).

The sail was woven first in the centre of the warp threads to form a triangle, which was left loose and not 'attached' to the sky. The sky, meanwhile, was woven across the remaining warp threads, skipping under the sail then out the other side. The blue threads were left loose on the back as illustrated, as since the piece would be hung on the wall, there would be no pressure or pulling on those threads. If the sail had been any wider, some kind of anchoring thread would have been necessary to the hold the blue threads in place.

Detail of the shell.

ABOVE *Reverse side of* **Galway Hooker** *(opposite), showing the blue threads loose behind the sail shape.*

LEFT **Galway Hooker**, *close-up showing boat shape in front of work.*

*Completed **Galway Hooker** by author with driftwood and braid.*

Elements of design in weaving

One of the joys of weaving is exploring the possibilities that result when we vary the raw materials. Colour, texture and thickness of yarns and fibres determine the overall finished look of the weaving. We can also control the design by building up horizontal rows, creating curves as we go.

The sequence of lifting threads across the row can be varied to form geometric designs in the actual weave. The best way to learn the variations possible in weaving is to try them out and see what pleases you.

OPPOSITE PAGE *Detail of the centre of a rug from Mexico, showing graphic lines which form curved shapes on the surface of the weave.*

LEFT *In this illustration the warp threads are lifted in a different sequence from plain weave to form a more complicated surface pattern. A stick shuttle is used to take the weft threads through the resulting shed. Photo: Pavel L/ Shutterstock.*

COLOUR

Rainbow

On several occasions I've woven a piece which was not the colour success I'd planned. While I tended towards despondency and failure, a customer would come in and be ecstatic because they had finally found the colour combination they'd been searching for and thank me profusely for creating it.

ABOVE LEFT *Rainbow hanks of yarn dyed with natural dyes on Arran to get as close as possible to a true rainbow spectrum.*

ABOVE **Rainbow** *weaving by author using natural-dyed Aran wool, braided finish, wooden beads and the occasional length of white silk for contrast and texture. Approximately 1 m x 30 cm.*

My biggest source of colour inspiration has always been the rainbow. On our island, it can be rainy and sunny at the same time and double rainbows are a common occurrence. I'm always on the lookout for the exact colour of yarn which could duplicate the nuances that occur between the solid colours in the rainbow to catch their elusive quality before they disappear. It's an exciting moment when I find what I'm looking for. The possibilities for colour in weaving are endless. There is a huge range of yarns and fibres available, from natural colours from sheep, alpaca and other animal and plant fibres, to an infinite palette of dyed yarns. (If you want to experiment with dying yarn yourself, see pages 81–7.)

Often a random selection of yarns will suggest the design of the weaving itself. Alternatively, choosing the yarns for an idea or a design will focus your thinking and suggest ways in which the design could be developed.

Finding inspiration for colour in weaving is a great reason to go for a walk on the beach, a stroll in the park, or out to observe what is all around and see how you can use what you see in your design.

Inspiration from the garden or park

For colour inspiration, nothing can beat the random combinations which appear from even the most uncoordinated garden or park. Nature throws colour together in a way that adults sometimes find intimidating, though children have no such inhibitions.

Pick a posy of flowers from your garden (or in the park, take some photos) and find some yarns that reflect the combination of colours – even the most basic striped weaves take on a magic of their own as they reflect a bit of daring and unusual arrangements in the stripes. It's up to you to create your own rainbow and to find your own colour challenges which feed your creative soul. There's no need to compare your choices or judge them by anyone else's standards. This is one of the magical areas of weaving where you can explore to your heart's content – you can build your own portfolio of colour ideas as you develop them. Sometimes colour is dictated by the materials you can find available; sometimes you have an idea of the colour combination you want to produce, then you may have to go on a fibre hunt, but this is usually a joyful experience.

Brodick Shore, Isle of Arran, Scotland.

When I teach workshops, I provide a big basket of yarns of various colours, shades, thicknesses and textures which I've collected, been given or found in our local charity shop. The different combinations and designs that result from a group of people using the same basket of yarns can be amazing; each individual has their own idea as to how the colours should be used.

It is often difficult to make the first choices in any creative process.

Being confronted by a multi-coloured basket can be as daunting as facing a blank canvas in painting, where the first move may be the most difficult in producing the finished piece.

Rainbow yarns with finished purses.

To make the initial selection process easier, I usually suggest that each person chooses three yarns of similar weight which they think work well together. These three colours alone can be used to produce a simple frame loom design. Usually though, ideas and discussions begin to flow and changes occur as part of the creative process. The initial confident choice of colours forms a base for creative development.

Once you have woven one or two pieces, there are several ways in which you can develop your own sense of colour and what works for you:

- Go to exhibitions and museums and see what other people have put together that appeals to you.

- Look around your immediate environment and see what nature puts together – startling combinations that wouldn't immediately occur to us.

- The sea has shades and nuances you've never thought of before; rocks and tree barks bring together colours unique to their geography; the sky takes on new possibilities to interpret in yarns and fibres.

Try weaving the same design in different colours and compare the effects.

Graphic design in weaving

There are many examples of the smooth graphic lines in tapestries where yarns of the same thickness and twist are used to great effect to depict floral backgrounds, pictures of daily domestic life and great historical events.

Tapestry-weaving, large and small, historical and modern, often incorporates a prescribed graphic design, known as the cartoon (see page 27), which is followed rigorously to produce the desired result. In this case the thickness of the yarn is calculated to fit the cartoon so that the design has the desired graphic lines to produce the finished woven picture. A cartoon can be used on a frame loom to create a small traditional tapestry, just as effectively as on a large studio loom.

CREATING GRAPHIC LINES WITH WEAVING

By using the ancient technique of interlocking you can create vertical and curved lines in the weave while working horizontally and building up the lines row by row.

Interlocking practice piece

The techniques below are easy to learn once you have mastered the ideas of weaving a few stripes and changing colour. To begin with, it is advisable to have only one interlocking halfway across the row until you feel comfortable with the technique.

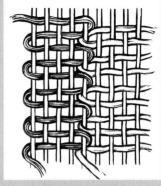

Basic interlocking. Here the horizontal rows are interlocked round the same weft thread to build up a vertical line in the weave.

1. Using either cotton warp thread or 3-ply Aran-weight yarn, set up the loom with 18 threads (9 on either side of the centre of the loom) following the instructions on pages 34–5 for warping-up and knotting.

2. Weave in two cardboard strips to form a base (or more if you would like the finished piece to have a longer fringe).

3. Choose three strong colours of Aran-weight yarn for this design: the interplay of simple shapes and colours will give a satisfying finished result.

Red, yellow and blue sampler.

Red, yellow and blue weaving in progress.

4. Weave 2 cm (¾ inch) plain weave in colour 1, following the basic instructions for starting off and changing colour on page 40.

5. Weave 5 cm (¼ inch) plain weave in colour 2.

6. Weave 2.5 cm (1 inch) plain weave in colour 1.

7. Find the centre of the loom.

8. Weave the first colour from one side of the warp (it doesn't matter whether it's right or left, whichever is more comfortable).

9. Leave a tail, as though you were changing colours to make a new stripe, and tuck this in by weaving over two threads and taking the tail through to the back.

10. Weave across to the centre space between threads 9 and 10.

11. Pick up the second colour from the other side. Weave across to the same point between threads 9 and 10. Leave a tail at the beginning edge as usual and tuck it through to the back the end two threads.

12. Loop the two shuttles round each other in the space between threads 9 and 10, and weave each one back to the edge.

13. It is important when interlocking rows to keep the tension of the weave consistent so that the surface is as even as possible, in other words don't pull the yarn too tight round the end threads. Keep a light touch.

14. Continue in this way until you've formed a square with both colours.

15. Finish with the shuttles at either edge. Cut the yarn, again leaving tails, and tuck these round the end two threads and through to the back.

16. Reversing the colours, follow the instructions above until you have two more squares, creating a chequerboard effect.

17. Switch to colour 1 and follow the instructions to weave a diagonal line, using colour 2 as background – or colour 3 if you prefer.

18. Once the diagonal line reaches the edge of the warp threads, weave a second diagonal line in the other direction to form a triangle as shown on the previous page. Weave a few rows to finish off, using one of the three colours, or add a fourth colour for interest.

19. Undo the warp at the top of the loom, leaving the loops to hang the piece.

20. Untie the knots and form loops the same length as the others, darning the remaining yarn invisibly down through the weave. Pull out the cardboard strips and trim the ends evenly at the bottom of the loom to form a fringe.

21. You should have 18 threads at the bottom. Tie these together in pairs to stop the work from unravelling.

LEFT *Interlocking to form geometric shapes.*

RIGHT *Interlocking to form 'steps'.*

INSPIRATION FROM A MEXICAN RUG

My awareness of weaving began in Mexico in 1968 when I attended Spanish summer courses in San Miguel de Allende in Guanajuato province. I was captivated. I bought a rug from a craft co-operative in Mexico City to remind me of my trip. Over the years, as the colours have faded, they've added a new dimension of softness, very beautiful in itself. As well as being a cosy and decorative part of our household for many years, it has provided design inspiration and illustrated weaving principles for me and my students. The illustrations here demonstrate how graphic lines and curves are achieved row by row as the weaving builds up horizontally.

Different techniques can be combined in the same weaving to form vertical, diagonal and curved shapes. Traditional tapestries are based on these simple variations, so practising them on the frame loom will prepare you for designing and weaving a larger piece. I've used photographs of the details on the rug to illustrate interlocking techniques. It is important at first with interlocking to use yarns of the same weight to build up the design. As you become more experienced, you can experiment with weights of yarn and types of interlocking to form a more textured surface.

If you look closely at the central black circle, you can see that the curves are formed by straight lines, woven closely together, moving across the warp threads to create the illusion of roundness. In the centre is the iconic picture of the eagle conquering the snake, a key image of Mexican and Central American culture and mythology. The homely addition of the cactus brings the flight down to earth, anchoring the eagle's talons, again on the horizontal with fine interlocking threads and slight gradations in the diagonals and curves. The more pictorial aspects of the rug such as the flower petals and flags are also worked horizontally, interlocking to create a solid weave.

Detail of Mexican rug showing centre seam. The rug is twice as wide as the loom it was woven on, so there is a finely stitched, almost invisible seam in the centre, carefully lined up with the design.

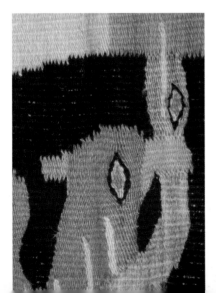
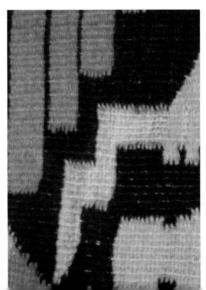

FAR LEFT *Straight lines interlocked to form curves and eye shapes.*

LEFT *Details of eagle and snake's head and snake's tail.*

Large rugs and tapestries can be broken down visually into their component parts. You can learn a lot about style and technique from observing a small figure or detail on an otherwise overwhelming woven piece. If you have access to a museum with a tapestry collection, it can be inspirational to look at the way the techniques were used traditionally to amazing effect. As you build your own portfolio of ideas it soon becomes evident how you can create your own individual designs using traditional techniques.

ABOVE *This diagram shows the formation of a triangle using interlocking. To form a diamond, weave a triangle on top of the first triangle, reversing the shaping. Interlocking triangles and diamonds form the cornerstone of traditional weaving designs in many parts of the world.*

ABOVE LEFT *This design features diamonds and other shapes created using interlocking.*

BELOW LEFT Two Grey Hills, *a Navajo rug, courtesy of Ute Mader, Miracle Design. Another design featuring diamonds and interlocking.*

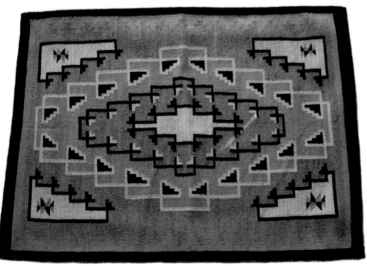

Project: Beach Hut *weaving*

Yarns for **Beach Hut**.

ABOVE, LEFT AND RIGHT *Stabilising cord.*

1. Using a larger frame loom with four grooves per inch, find the centre of the loom and count eight spaces in from the left-hand side. Attach the warp to the loom, using the knot illustrated on page 35.

2. Wind the warp from top to bottom until you have 32 threads, then tie off using the same knot as before.

3. Weave in three strips of cardboard 2.5 cm (1 inch) wide so that there will be enough warp to make a fringe at the bottom when the weaving is finished. If you wish, you can weave in a cord and tie it on each side of the frame to stabilise the warp threads at the point you will start weaving. You can untie this later.

4. Weave your chosen weft to represent the sea and beach for 12.5 cm (5 inches), then begin to interlock the weave using three shuttles. The two sides will be the same yarn, with the white beach hut in the middle.

5. To start the row, weave to the eighth thread with the right-hand shuttle.

Basic weaving with found objects from the beach.

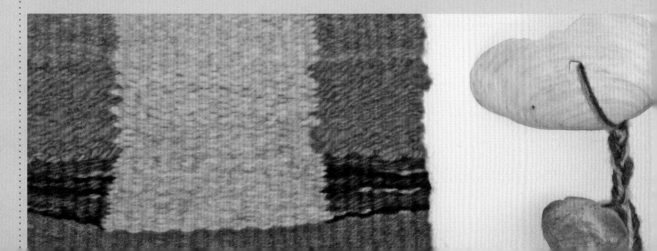

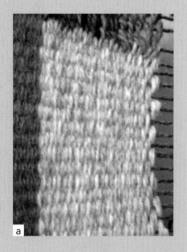
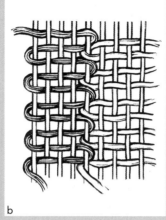

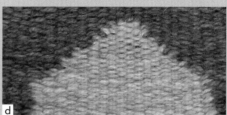

a

b

c

d

6. Weave 16 threads with the 'beach hut' shuttle.

7. Weave from the edge to the eighth thread with the left-hand shuttle.

8. Interlock round the eighth thread on each side and weave back to the edges.

9. Continue in this way to form the beach hut as follows:
   * beach yarns on either side: 2.5 cm (1 inch)
   * sea yarns on either side: 5 cm (2 inches)
   * change the side shuttles to the colour you've chosen for the sky.
   * sky yarns on either side: 5 cm (2 inches)

10. Continue with these two colours interlocking diagonally to form the roof of the beach hut with the sky on either side, ending with the sky shuttles on either edge of the weave.

11. Thread a length of wood or driftwood a few inches wider than the weaving through the loops. Untie the knots on either end and form two more loops the same length as the others, then darn the remaining yarn invisibly along the edge of the weaving for 5 cm (2 inches), anchoring with a backstitch.

12. The bottom fringe can be plaited or decorated with beads or shells with holes threaded through and tied loosely. Finish off by twisting or plaiting a few strands of yarn from the colours in the weaving into a cord. Loop onto either side of the wood.

a. *Basic interlocking techniques to form* **Beach Hut**.

b. *Basic interlocking. By alternately winding the horizontal weft threads around the vertical, a straight line is formed. Once you begin interlocking round a central vertical thread, you weave row by row with one colour at a time. For example, for this project you weave green or black to represent the shore, white to represent the hut and green or black to represent the other side of the shore. This builds up a pattern of colour that you can change at any time.*

c. *Forming a triangle with interlocking.*

d. **Beach Hut** *diagonal interlocking.*

RIGHT *Finished* **Beach Hut** *by author with shells, sea urchin case and driftwood holder.*

CREATING TEXTURE

Yarn and fibre offer an added dimension to the possibilities of weaving design. Thickness, texture and twist all contribute to the look of a finished piece, and texture may well be the most exciting characteristic of yarn and weaving.

If you want to try out your ideas before putting them on the loom, you could wind a few of your planned warp threads around a small piece of sturdy cardboard. Then, using a large needle threaded with the weft, weave a few rows to see whether you like the effect. That way, you can see how the colours and textures work together. Try different combinations and widths of stripes in this way to give you inspiration, before embarking on weaving your preferred version on the loom.

RECYCLED CLOTH STRIPS

Known as 'rags' in the tradition of hooked or woven rugs, strips of cloth can take the place of yarns in weft to provide colour and added texture and a sturdy weave for household use. Recycling in this way not only contributes to a greener existence but gives the cloth a new lease of life and reveals new textures and threads which may not have been evident in the original cloth. You can practise weaving small samples on the frame loom, trying out various textures and thicknesses in anticipation of someday weaving a rug.

The best way to cut a piece of cloth for weaving is to start at the bottom edge. With a sharp pair of scissors and lots of patience, cut a 1.25 cm (½ inch) strip across the material, stopping just before you cut right to the opposite edge, then turn the material 90° and cut right round the

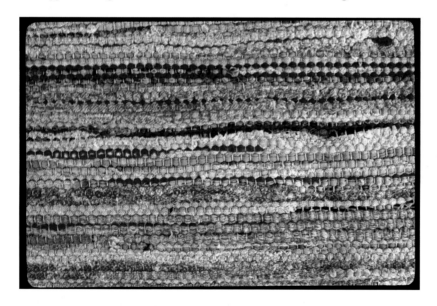

The 'rags' in this sample are from various recycled clothes from my wardrobe in the early 70s. I still have the rug with all the memories and those 'rags' are very precious.

edges of the cloth, going in ever-decreasing circles until you reach the centre. Don't worry about being too exact: any slight differences in width will add texture to the weave. Likewise, the corners form an interesting texture in the weaving if they are left untrimmed.

The triangles that are formed in each corner from cutting this way can become part of the weaving design, or you can trim them off so that the corner strip matches the rest of your 'rag' in width. By cutting in a continuous strip, you avoid having to join cloth edges, which can make the weave bulky or lumpy.

SCULPTURAL WEAVING

At the other extreme from smooth graphic design are weavings which use twisted yarns and textures, incorporating metal fibres and found objects to create pieces which could be defined as sculptures as much as weavings.

Grasses, driftwood from the beach and old rusty nails are but a few of the textures that can be combined with yarn to produce your own particular interpretation. Again, the secret is to look around and see what combinations are possible and incorporate them into your own work. If you enjoy working with found-object looms, especially when they are three dimensional, you will soon see the relationship between weaving and sculpture and the possibilities that weaving has for using different media such as paper strips or metal threads.

BELOW LEFT *Sculptural weaving incorporating razor shell and seaweed from the beach, mixed with yarns which echo the colours of the shore.*

RIGHT *Mirroring. Using the frame loom, you can weave stripes in different colours until you reach the centre of the weave, then simply reverse the colour arrangement in the second half to mirror what you've done in the first. If you vary the width of the stripes, rather than weaving them to equal measurements, this will create a much more interesting pattern, especially when reversed on the top half.*

Developing the weave that suits your design best

One of the most rewarding aspects of weaving is the process of learning to combine yarns and fibres in the warp and weft to achieve exactly the result you want. You can experiment on a frame loom to begin with, extending possibilities as your skills increase and your eye determines what is most pleasing.

WEAVE STRUCTURE AND PATTERN DRAFTS

The subject of weave structure could fill several volumes on its own. Patterns for weave structure are called drafts, and can be found in many books on weaving, or on the variations in weaving design.

The best way to understand a weaving draft is to weave a sample and see how the threads interact with each other. Reading drafts becomes an easier task and you will find yourself on a new journey of possibilities, limited only by the type of loom you have and its capacity for lifting more than one warp thread at a time.

We can learn a considerable amount about weave structure by working on the frame loom. Weaving is based on mathematics. (Don't be put off by this.) In its simplest form on a frame loom, every other thread is lifted in the first row. In the second row the threads which were down are lifted, and it is this alternating sequence which gives the weave its strength and structure. This is known as plain weave. This is the simplest of all the weaves, but the formula for more complicated weaves is the same, i.e. the draft shows the over-under sequence for the weft thread covering the warp and the look of the pattern over several rows of weaving.

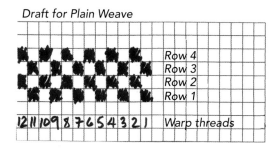

Draft for Plain Weave

The draft shown here is for plain weave with 12 warp threads set up on the frame loom. The dark squares represent the weft thread going over the warp; the blank spaces represent the weft thread going under the warp. The draft on paper is smaller in scale than the actual woven sample.

BALANCE BETWEEN WARP AND WEFT

There are basically three types of balance in the weave, depending on how you set up your loom. You can practise controlling these on the frame loom to see how they work.

As you weave, you can see both threads equally on the surface of the weave, giving the balanced look that we usually think of when we talk about weaving. The colours blend evenly too, creating a third shade which is a visual mixture of the warp and weft. This is a very powerful design tool in weaving, an effect not easily created in other media.

If you were to space your threads every 2.5 cm (1inch) instead of every 1.25 cm (½ inch), i.e. every other groove on the frame loom, the weft would cover the warp threads, giving what we call a weft-face weave, where the warp is hidden, apart from the top and bottom fringes on the loom. This also happens with 1.25 cm (½ inch) warp spacing, if you use a finer warp thread than weft.

LEFT *Example of plain weave. This type of balanced weave occurs when the weft threads are the same thickness as the warp threads. Photo: Fribus Ekaterina/ Shutterstock.*

RIGHT *Twill weave.*

LANDSCAPES

Wherever you are, you can find inspiration from looking at the shapes, forms and colours that make up the surrounding area. In town, you can create building scapes using the basic *Beach Hut* design (see pages 57–9) with vertical and diagonal interlocking, working with strong shapes and colour. In more natural surroundings, inspiration comes from the curves and profiles of the landscape.

If you're not confident with sketching and painting, weaving and fibre offer you another means of expressing what you see around you, adding your own interpretation as you go. Writing short descriptions of a landscape idea or composing a short poem can help you visualise a weaving. Again, weaving becomes the catalyst for personal creative development in a way that might otherwise not have been possible.

The photos here were inspired by a precious moment in my life: *Road to King's Caves* captures a moment on a walk along the west coast of Arran one sparkling summer day. The colours were unbelievably psychedelic in the clear sunshine and the sea was very blue and still. When I look at this weaving now, I see myself striding along the forest path, high above the sea, trying to keep up with my long-legged sons, on a rare occasion when we were all together. The weaving starts in one corner by shaping a curve to reflect the contour of the landscape. By adding another curved section from the other side, the weaving begins to take shape.

With a bit of practice you begin to feel how the curves will fit together and each piece you weave will provide inspiration and instruction for the next one. Once you understand the principles of interlocking, and you are able to weave a flat even surface with no unwanted gaps, you can begin to build your weave more freely, combining basic interlocking, creating curves then straightening the rows again to create a horizontal effect. This usually takes more than one shuttle across the row, but again experience and practice are the best ways to learn how this all works.

In this weaving all the yarns are the same weight and thickness, doubled round the shuttle to create an even thicker, more multicoloured yarn which in turn gives a more complete impression of the colours of that day.

ABOVE *Interlocking by dovetailing. Interlocking happens with more than one thread at a time, as in this illustration of dovetailing. Weave back and forth a few rows at a time and interlock as in the illustration. This will push the yarn down and form gentle curves as the weaving progresses.*

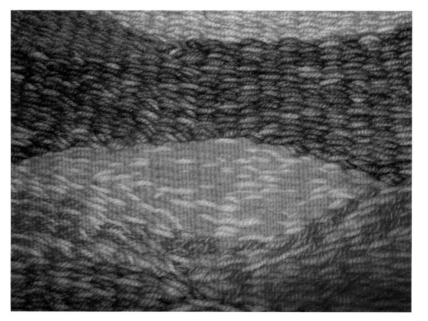

LEFT *In this detail of the work opposite you can see how the landscape curves fit into each other. The blue of the sky is woven across the row, following the curves but gradually becoming more flat and even as the weaving progresses.*

OPPOSITE Road to King's Caves *(2003), by author. Warp: 12/9 cotton warp yarn; weft: natural-dyed Aran-weight yarn.*

Your personal portfolio

Weaving can be an artistic catalyst at any age or level of experience. Before I learned to weave, I thought of myself as an 'academic' with no artistic inclination. Weaving made me look at colour combinations in a much more careful way. It also developed my drawing skills, as planning a design before starting to weave sometimes made it necessary to draw things on paper as a guide. I soon discovered that I enjoyed the process of experimenting with colour and drafting ideas on paper. While I still prefer to express my own creativity by actually weaving, I now have a collection of notebooks with sketches and samples which stand alone as artistic objects in themselves.

BELOW *Create a sketchbook of scenes that appeal to you to use as inspiration for weaving. Photo: BMJ/Shutterstock.*

OPPOSITE PAGE *Photo: Shebeko/ Shutterstock.*

Quick sketches

I find quick sketches without too much detail work best for me. I can then look at the areas in the sketch and decide how to create the effect I want. I don't often draw anything more elaborate before I start weaving: for me, weaving is the easiest way to express myself artistically.

Sometimes I'll use a watercolour or a drawing I've done and interpret it in weaving, but even then I take only the essential ideas and by the time they reach the loom they are transformed into a tapestry, rather than a copy of my drawing or painting.

There are examples where paintings have been copied line by line into a tapestry in professional studios. While I admire the effort and the result, I personally feel that the paintings are complete in themselves. We have so many options for design with simple looms and raw materials, I prefer to explore these creatively rather than duplicate something which is already beautiful and perfect.

In this book I want to give you confidence by starting off with projects which have complete instructions. The idea is to take those and develop your own ideas and try them out. In the long run, it's much more satisfying to create your own designs and carry them through to completed woven pieces. I learned to weave on a course where structure was extremely controlled, and I'll always be grateful for that. However, as I began to understand how weaving structure worked, I was able to develop my own ideas.

The idea of creating designs can strike fear into the heart of the most competent and skilled craftsperson, especially when it comes to textile crafts, which most of us learned by tracing and copying rather than starting from first principles. A design is made up of its component parts. Once you have learned a few basic weaving techniques, you can combine them to build your own composition.

THE BLETHERS

The idea for the tapestry shown opposite came to me one morning, heading for work on the underground in Stockholm. Across from me there were two ladies of a certain age, who reminded me instantly of my Scottish Granny and her friend Nanny Rogers. The women were speaking rapidly in Finnish and although I couldn't understand a word, I knew exactly what they were saying: '…and she said to me, and I said to her, you just cannot believe … and what he said to her.' I never heard the end of the conversation, but they were speaking the universal language of women everywhere putting the world to rights, which in Scotland is known as 'blethering', so this tapestry is a tribute to blethers everywhere.

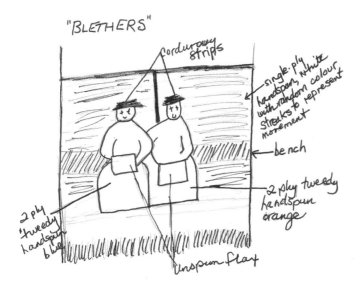

The following labels appear on the sketch:

"BLETHERS"

corduroy strips

single ply handspun white with random colour streaks to represent movement

bench

2 ply tweedy handspun orange

2 ply tweedy handspun blue

unspun flax

The Blethers, *sketch by author.*

The Blethers *(1981) by author.*

The quick sketch was to remind me of their tweed coats, sensible hats and sturdy shopping bags, with the carriage window and its moving light showing behind them. The next step was to choose yarns and fibres which would bring out the shapes and textures in the finished piece.

Rather than use a cartoon (see page 27), I marked the important points of the drawing directly on the warp with a permanent marker pen. This was possible because the weft threads would cover the warp according to the spacing I'd used. By using the dots as a rough guide, I could weave freely between them, creating the effects I wanted as I worked.

I used smooth, hand-spun single-ply random-dyed yarn for the background with colours streaking across to create the effect of a swiftly moving background. The coats were woven with 2-ply textured hand-spun yarn to represent tweed. The hats were woven from corduroy cloth cut into narrow strips to give a bulky look and the faces were worked in fine flesh-coloured wool. The only place I cheated was in embroidering the eyes and mouth with simple stitches. (I didn't realise until much later, but the faces and hats owe some inspiration to LEGO® figures which at that time could be found in most corners of the house as they were my children's favourite toy.)

The shopping bags were woven in relief from unspun linen fibres. In the space between the bag and the main weaving I placed a muslin pouch with dried herbs to keep the moths away. The tapestry interlocking techniques between the background and the figures was worked row by row, creating added texture where the yarn in the coats was sometimes slightly thicker than the background.

Creating a scrapbook

One of the most valuable tools you can develop as you experiment with weaving is a scrapbook where you record what you do, along with some notes about whether it was successful or what you would do next time. Remember that each piece is a practice for the next piece, and as weaving is an ongoing journey, there may be no such thing as a masterpiece.

This is also good practice for record-keeping if you decide to pursue weaving with a more complicated loom where written patterns and drafts are essential. You can use some of the pages as a scrapbook for collecting design ideas and colour combinations that appeal to you, to use as inspiration when planning your own work. I find that a spiral-bound A4 sketchbook is ideal for recording weaving projects. I use a hole punch along the side to loop through yarn samples from warp and weft, so that I can remember exactly what I did.

Here are some of the things you should record as a reference. As you go along, you may think of other things you want to add to the list.

- name of project

- rough sketch or notes of ideas

- approximate finished size

- type of loom

- yarns for warp and weft: record detailed information about the yarns, better still paste a label into your book so that you remember what to order next time

- warp spacing (in the case of the frame looms 1, 2 or 4 warps per inch)

- weft yarns

- photo of finished piece

- comments – what you liked and didn't like

- ideas for next time

You'll be amazed at how often you look back at these initial ideas and develop them in your weaving over time.

Author's sketchbook notes for Beach Hut.

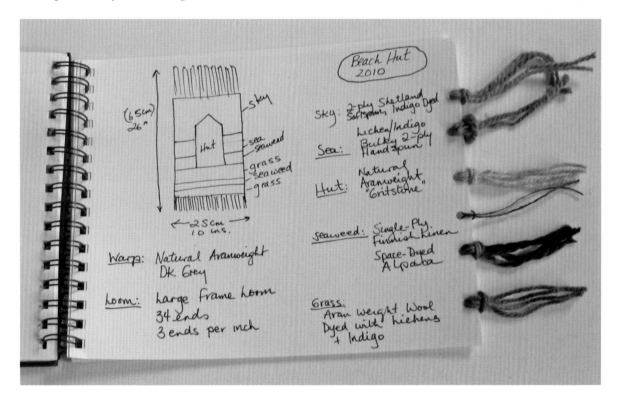

Choosing and preparing fibres and yarns

In choosing fibres and yarns for weaving, there are a few things to consider along with colourfastness and suitability for the design. Environmental issues are paramount: it is important to choose fibres and dyes from renewable sources. It is also important to choose yarns which are environmentally friendly in the production process and don't pollute the earth or water with residual chemicals when the dyebath is exhausted of colour and is discarded.

LEFT *Close-up of Ecuadorian weaving found in a village market by the author in 2003. 92 x 92 cm. This wonderful weaving is from a project in a village near Ambato in Ecuador. It has been carefully planned so that the colours form the desired pattern, beautifully co-ordinated to depict the people and their village. The weft threads are extra fine, to hold the design in place. Although they contribute to the woven appearance, they are a neutral colour so the design in the unspun yarns is prevalent.*

OPPOSITE PAGE *This wooden loom is used to produce traditional Arabic rugs. The yarns are used in a range of colour combinations. Photo: dotshock/Shutterstock.*

We should also consider how the yarns we use are produced and if possible should use raw materials which are both sustainable to the environment and take into consideration labour resources and lack of exploitation. Charity shops are a great source of recycled yarn, which is especially useful in creating variety in a beginners' workshop basket.

The crafts of spinning and dyeing are inextricably linked with weaving, providing the colour and fibre which will determine the final design of the weave. Sometimes I set out with the idea of producing enough of a certain thickness of yarn to complete a specific project. When I look back on my own experience, it was this fascination with being able to control the final result that inspired me to learn to spin and dye with natural materials.

More often, the weaving takes shape from the yarns that come about from 'experimenting' with spinning and dyeing. If you are the type of person who likes to experiment, then don't be put off by people who like to plan from the beginning. As you increase in confidence you will notice that the gap between raw materials and final result begins to close as you find your own individual style.

Natural fibres

WOOL FROM SHEEP, LLAMAS AND ALPACA

Wool comes in a range of natural colours from black to pale tan. White wool or pale shades of grey or tan lend themselves well to dyeing with natural dyes, or synthetic dyes with safe ingredients.

SILK

There are two kinds of silk fibre, both from the silk moth (*Bombyx mori*), which feeds on mulberry trees. There is cultivated silk, where the moth cocoons are unwound and the resulting silk thread is used with its natural strength. There is also wild silk, where the moth grub breaks out of the cocoon, leaving the case behind. The fibre is usually white or tussah, a beautiful creamy colour. You can dye silk with certain dyes, but it is so beautiful in its natural state that it's a difficult choice to alter it.

FLAX

Flax or linen is the product of the stalk of the flax plant (*Linum usitatissimum*), which grows very tall in climates such as Scotland and Ireland, where there is plenty of moisture in the air. The process of turning flax into linen is time-consuming but well worth the effort for the finished result.

Natural Shetland wool colours.

 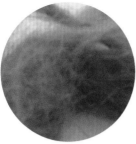 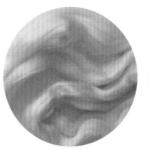 

FROM LEFT
Grey Shetland sheep's wool.
Alpaca from Peru.
White silk fibres.
Linen fibres from the flax stalk.

OTHER NATURAL FIBRES

Cotton is produced in various parts of the world where the climate is suitable. Although I prefer to use fibres which are available locally, I order cotton yarn from reliable sources, mostly for making warps. The process of separating the cotton from the stalks of the plant is more labour-intensive than processing wool or silk, but the resulting fibre can be spun into fine, strong threads which are suitable for many types of woven cloth.

In Scandinavia, cloth is still made from nettles processed in the same way as flax, taking care in the picking of them. In Lesotho, goat's hair is spun into mohair and in some countries cow hair is used to produce rug yarn.

 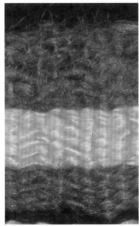

FAR LEFT *Weaving sample with unspun flax, alpaca and silk on a 2-ply cashmere/silk blend warp. Woven on a small frame loom with 12 warp threads. Length: weaving 25 cm, top fringe 12.5 cm, bottom fringe 16 cm; width 12 cm.*

LEFT *Unspun fibres weaving sample (detail). The silk, linen and alpaca were twisted gently so they held together during weaving. The fabric gains strength once the unspun fibres have formed a web with the 2-ply yarn in the warp. This technique lends itself well to soft rugs and cushions.*

Yarns

Yarns are distinguished from each other by the following characteristics:

- *Fibre* – for example, natural or synthetic, dyed or undyed. Some fibres are more elastic than others, which gives them different characteristics when they are spun. This adds to the texture of the finished weaving and is an important feature which influences the final design.

- *Preparation* – how the fibres have been blended or dyed before spinning. This influences the pattern in the yarn.

- *Thickness* – this is determined by how many metre (or yards) of yarn can be measured in a gram (or an ounce). In commercial terms, yarns have been graded by concepts like Aran-weight wool, or 'chunky', but the basic premise is the same – each yarn consists of one or more threads spun in varying thicknesses, either clockwise or anti-clockwise.

- *Ply* – the number of threads of fibre which are spun together to make the yarn. The individual threads are 'plied' or twisted together on a spinning wheel or an industrial wheel. The possibilities of spinning plus the possibilities of plying are only limited by the thickness of the opening on the spinning wheel which the yarn feeds through as it is twisted. Note that ply does not necessarily determine thickness. It is possible to have a very thin 2-ply yarn or a very thick 2-ply yarn, as shown in the photo below left.

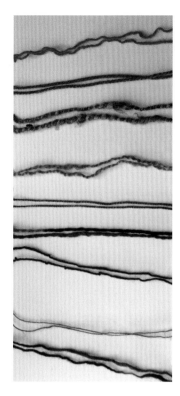

Examples of spun and plied yarns.

Difference between ply and thickness – there are two examples of 2-ply yarns here, different in thickness. The finer yarn on the right is 3-ply, made up of finer single-ply yarns than the other two.

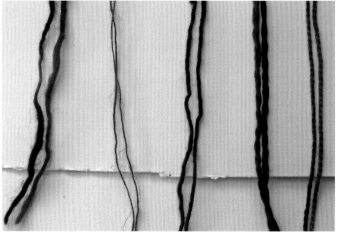

Samples showing difference between thickness and ply. Left to right:
1. Single-ply Peruvian alpaca.
2. Fine single-ply linen from Finland.
3. Single-ply wool from Sweden.
4. 2-ply alpaca, dyed before spinning to create a random colour effect.
5. 2-ply linen, silk and seaweed-based yarn.

- *Twist* – there are two possible directions to spin yarn: clockwise and anti-clockwise. The direction affects the way the light reflects on the surface of the finished weave, creating another dimension to the final look. You can create a weaving from the same fibre, spun in different directions, giving different appearances.

Twist is especially important when choosing suitable yarns for warp and weft. Bearing in mind that the warp must be robust and elastic enough to hold the tension as it is wound around the loom, the yarn used for the warp must be stronger than the yarns used for the weft, which are held in place as soon as they are woven in. An example of this is the use of unspun fibres in the project described on page 38, held in place by a 2-ply cashmere/silk blend, which would not be strong enough if the fibres were unspun.

Left to right:
1. 2-ply hand-spun wool, dyed with traditional madder.
2. Hand-spun chunky 2-ply soft grey Shetland.
3. 3-ply alpaca.
4. 3-ply Aran-weight wool.

SPINNING

Spinning gives fibre strength as it is turned into yarn. The drop spindle is a traditional tool that is used to twist fibre into yarn. Drop spindles were usually made of clay with a hole for a piece of wood. These clay pieces are known as whorls. (For an example of a contemporary handmade spindle, see page 93.)

These spindle whorls date from the fifth to the first century BC. Photo: Semester/Shutterstock.

This spindle has a groove carved at the top of the wood to stop the wool from slipping. Photo: Moritorus/Shutterstock.

This spinner operates a modern wheel that holds the equivalent of the spindle. The art of spinning is to co-ordinate the speed of the twist with drawing out the right amount of fibre for the thickness of yarn. As with weaving, the skills of spinning are best learned from an expert, first of all observing and then gradually learning to balance all the moves that turn 'straw into gold'. Photo: joyfuldesigns/ Shutterstock.

USING UNSPUN FIBRES

Unspun fibres have a texture and lustre that can be used to advantage if woven without twisting into a yarn. Wool especially can be dyed successfully in the fleece, giving interesting colour variations and subtle blends which are lost in spinning.

YARN WEIGHTS AND COUNTS

Traditionally, the thickness of yarns was identified by what was known as the count. This number referred to the number of yards per ounce or pound of yarn – in the metric system metres per gram or kilogram. The count of yarn spun by hand was done by winding the yarn off the spinning-wheel bobbin onto a simple rotating device called a skeiner.

The arms of the skeiner were usually 12 inches apart, forming a hank 2 yards around. The traditional skeiner had a simple clicking mechanism in the centre which counted the yards as the skeiner turned, though the operator had to pay attention and count the clicks as the early devices had no automatic counting system.

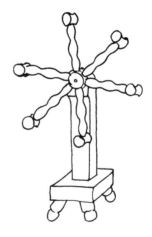

Traditional skeiner.

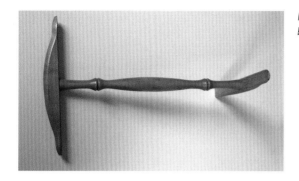

Niddy-noddy, with 46 cm between crossbars.

A niddy-noddy is a similar device, but simpler. When the yarn is wound once round the niddy-noddy it will be two yards around. When the hank is taken off the niddy-noddy and weighed, the yarn can then be counted as follows:

1. Count the number of yards on one side of the hank.

2. Multiply by two to get the total number of metres or yards in the hank – based on the fact that the hank is 2 metres around.

3. Divide the number of metres (or yards) by the number of grams (or ounces in the hank).

The result will be the count of the yarn in grams per metre or yards per ounce. An extra notation was usually added to the yarn count to indicate how many threads or plies formed the spun yarn. For example, if the yarn was made up of two spun threads which had been plied together, the notation /2 was used in the count. So if you had 20 yards per ounce of 2-ply yarn, the count would be 20/2. The higher the count, the finer the yarn, and the number indicating the ply simply tells how many threads make up the yarn.

As you build your portfolio, it's important to keep a record of the count of the yarn that you use for each project. As you gain experience, you can choose which thickness of yarn will be most suitable for each project you plan. When you order yarn, you will find that the count is often marked on the label. If not, then by all means ask the manufacturer so that you know what you are working with.

Sometimes yarns will be referred to by their traditional name such as Aran-type wool or cotton rug warp. You can still check the count on the niddy-noddy by following the instructions above, and work out for yourself which other yarns are of similar weight and count, which is useful for planning projects. A small frame loom is ideal for experimenting with these concepts.

AFTER ICELAND

After Iceland records a moment on a bus trip from the north of the country to Reykjavik on a short November day, after a work session in Holar with other members of an international team. One of the stops we made was at the bottom of a glacier at Barnafoss, about 100 km from Reykjavik.

Melted ice pours through the lava rock, making it more porous as time goes on, tumbling into the pool below. To capture the images and colours, I visited the yarn store in Reykjavik when we returned to the city, and chose chunky Icelandic wool with which to replicate the feelings and shades of that amazing scene.

Unspun white silk woven at random along the edge of the curves formed by the weaving replicated the water tumbling through the rock. This weaving is an example where curves and more formal interlocking were used together to create the required shapes.

ABOVE **After Iceland** *(2002), by author.*

LEFT **After Iceland** *(detail).*

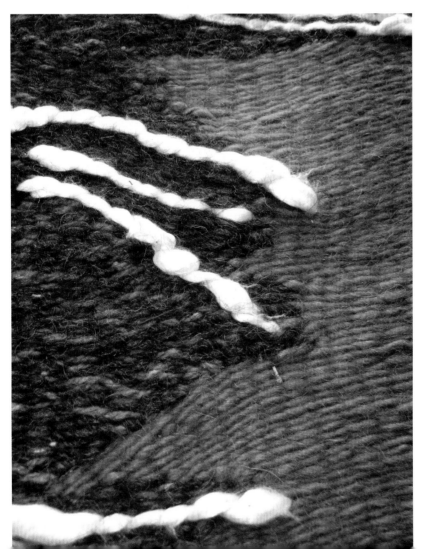

The dye process

I've included some notes here from my experiments with natural dye materials which led to the development of my own spectrum of natural dyes, which I call the Arran rainbow. All of these recipes are as safe as possible for the weaver and the environment, as long as you follow the few simple rules that are outlined below.

Though the results you get from following the recipes may not be what you expect, I hope this will start you on an exploration of what can be done with the natural resources in your local area. As with weaving, keeping notes of recipes, successes and failures will give you a portfolio of ideas to follow.

DYEING

Dyeing is best done in a studio using a dedicated cooker or hotplate, rather than in the kitchen. Outdoors on a campfire also works well, and also contributes to the atmosphere and experience of observing the fibres take on colour.

EQUIPMENT

- rubber gloves
- face mask if you are sensitive to fumes or powders
- scales, preferably ones where the container can be thoroughly cleaned after use – you may want to have a separate container for weighing indigo as the powder can easily stain
- stainless-steel pot or bucket with lid, for mordanting and dyeing (other metals tend to react with the chemicals and change the colour produced by the dyes)
- stainless-steel stirring rods or spoons
- thermometer which reaches the bottom of the pot and still allows you to take a temperature reading above the surface of the liquid
- glass measuring jar
- glass jars or plastic storage containers to store mordants and dyes (these should be stored in a cool, dark place)
- large jars to store dyebaths that you may want to reuse
- strong cotton string (leftover warp ends from weaving are ideal for tying hanks to stop them from tangling in the dyepot)

PREPARING FLEECE AND YARN FOR DYEING

Fleece and yarn should be washed in such a way that they keep their qualities of insulation and waterproofing. It is possible to wash all these items in the wool cycle of an automatic washing machine, as the temperature is controlled and the spin cycle is gentle. For fleece that is not particularly greasy or dirty, a mild, environmentally friendly dishwashing liquid or soap solution will clean the wool sufficiently. Soak for 20 minutes in lukewarm water, rinse and squeeze gently.

GENERAL HINTS FOR DYEING WITH NATURAL MATERIALS

- Work in a well ventilated room.
- Wear rubber gloves to protect the skin.
- Use stainless-steel pots or buckets and glass stirring rods if possible.
- Plants may be collected and dried for use out of season. When dyeing with fresh material, the weight of plant material should be twice the weight of the fibre to be dyed. Dried plants should be used in equal weight to the amount of fibre.

Wool should be prepared in hanks to allow the dye to flow freely among the fibres. Tie the hanks loosely in four places (top, bottom and both sides) with white wool or cotton. This will prevent tangling and make winding into balls easier after dyeing.

- For an even dye, use enough water to cover the wool in the container and leave enough room to stir the wool gently for the first 10 minutes.

- Always raise the temperature of the dye pot slowly to avoid damage to the fibre, and let the fibre cool down before washing.

- Always wet the fibre before putting it into the dye or mordant; this ensures an even distribution of dye throughout the wool.

It is important that the water is not too acidic when using natural dye materials, otherwise the colours can be affected and may wash out completely after dyeing. If in doubt, use a pH stick and check the water is neutral (pH 7).

MORDANTS

In order for wool to absorb plant dyes, it is often necessary to prepare it with chemicals known as mordants. The most common traditional mordants are alum and cream of tartar, ferrous and copper sulphate and potassium dichromate (chrome). These metallic salts also change the shade of the dye and can be used to 'sadden' or modify the colour.

Considering new health and safety recommendations, it is best to use just alum and cream of tartar, as the other traditional mordants can be hazardous in contact with the skin or in the fumes from the dye pot. Small quantities are acceptable if they are used with care, apart from chrome, which has been found to be carcinogenic.

TO MORDANT 450 GRAMS (16 OZ) OF WOOL

- 80g (3 oz) alum
- 20g (¾ oz) cream of tartar

1. Fill a stainless-steel bucket or pan with enough mordant solution to completely submerge the wool.
2. Bring slowly to 90°C and simmer for 1 hour, making sure that the liquid never reaches boiling point.
3. Leave to cool and squeeze gently to remove excess moisture. Hang to dry, preferably outdoors or in a well ventilated room. Once the fibre is dry you can store mordanted yarn in a cool, dark space for several months. Make sure you soak it thoroughly when ready to use in the dyepot.

THE ARRAN RAINBOW

My spectrum of natural dyes is inspired by the Arran rainbow.

Yellow

The truest yellow for a rainbow spectrum from natural dyes with pH neutral water is from dyer's weld (*Reseda luteola*). You may want to experiment with other local dyes; the procedure is the same for most plants yielding yellow.

Arran plants that give a good, fast colour are:

- birch leaves,
- St John's Wort (*Hypericum perforatum* – pick before flowering)
- heather – any kind (tips only, collected before or after flowering)
- bog myrtle (*Myrica gale*)

PROCEDURE WITH MORDANTED WOOL

1. For fresh plants, use twice as much plant material as wool; for dried plants, use equal weight of plants and wool.

2. Boil plant material for 2 hours to extract dye.

3. Simmer at 90°C for 1 hour.

4. Allow to cool.

5. Rinse fibre thoroughly.

Alternatively, place plant material, fibre and mordant together in a large pot and bring up to 90°C. Proceed from step 3 above.

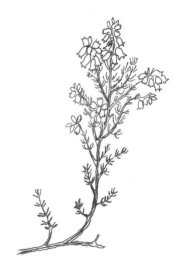

Bell heather. Drawing by Sabrina Sangster.

Birch leaves. Drawing by Sabrina Sangster.

Orange

Traditionally in the Scottish islands, ladies' bedstraw (*Galium verum*) was the plant of choice for dyeing orange. However, rumour has it that in the eighteenth century so much was being harvested from the wild that the plant was becoming extinct. A law was passed in the Scottish parliament that picking ladies' bedstraw was punishable by death. Although this may not be the law any more, it seems much safer to use madder root (*Rubia tinctorum*).

For 450 g (1 lb) of woollen yarn or fleece, pre-soaked to help it absorb the dye immediately, you will need:

- 450g (1 lb) madder
- 80g (3 oz) alum
- 20g (¾ oz) cream of tartar

PROCEDURE

1. Soak madder overnight.

2. Place in a bucket with wetted wool and mordants well diluted. Bring slowly to 90°C and simmer for 1 hour.

3. Let stand overnight to cool, if possible, and rinse carefully. Madder powder or particles usually shake out quite easily once the wool or fleece is dry.

This dye bath may be reused until the colour is exhausted.

In Scotland, it is difficult to get a true rainbow orange from natural dyes, but if you make sure the water is pH neutral and the madder is from a reliable source, you should come very close.

Red

To obtain red, you can use cochineal. This is the dried bodies of the cactus beetle or louse (*Dactylopius coccus cacti*), which comes originally from South America but is also found in the Canary Islands, where the cacti on which the beetle lives are cultivated for the dye industry. The pure colour is sold as 'carmine' and is still used to dye military uniforms bright red.

To obtain purple-red from cochineal, first mordant the wool with alum and cream of tartar. The dried beetles are usually purchased whole and ground in a coffee grinder or pestle and mortar before dyeing.

To dye 450 grams (1 lb) of mordanted wool, use 80g (3 oz) cochineal powder. The dye bath may be used two or three times until the colour is exhausted. Be sure to use mordanted wool in the second and third baths.

BELOW *Dye stall in market, Cuzco, Peru. Merchandise includes natural cochineal and indigo. Photograph courtesy of Simon Ross-Gill.*

PROCEDURE

1. Soak cochineal powder overnight in enough water to dissolve all the powder.

2. Bring cochineal solution to the boil and boil vigorously for 20 minutes.

3. Top up with cool water and add the wet alum-mordanted wool. Add more water if necessary to cover wool.

4. Bring the temperature back to 90°C and simmer for 45 minutes.

5. Allow the mixture to cool before rinsing the wool.

> Take care – wear rubber gloves, and do not breathe in fumes while the mixture is boiling.

For bright red:

1. Do not use pre-mordanted wool. Soak the cochineal powder overnight as for purple.

2. Before bringing to the boil, add 15 g (½ oz) stannous chloride crystals and 28 g (1 oz) cream of tartar.

3. Add the wet unmordanted wool and proceed as for purple.

> Remember to add the caustic soda to the water and not the other way round, to avoid spattering.

Indigo

Indigo (*Indigofera tinctoria*) is a shrub belonging to the pea family. It has tiny reddish flowers and oval leaves. Fermentation of the leaves provides a blue dye powder, which can be processed to produce colour in natural fibres in contact with oxygen in the air. If the plant doesn't grow locally, natural indigo powder is available commercially.

If the procedure below is followed carefully, the dye will be colour and light fast. In the beginning some dye may rub off the fabric, but this usually settles with the first washing.

The first step in dyeing with indigo is to prepare the stock solution. This is added to the dyebath as explained below. If the dyebath is kept warm, there will be enough for at least one pound of wool fibre and more if lighter shades are acceptable. Apart from taking care to put the ingredients together in the right order, there is room for experimentation as to the best way to use the indigo stock and dyebath.

THE STOCK RECIPE

- 15g (½ oz) indigo
- 2.5 decilitre (a good cupful) water at 50°C
- 1 tbsp. caustic soda (NaOH)
- 13g (½ oz) sodium dithionite (Na_2S_2O4) – often sold under a brand name

Indigo plant. Drawing by Sabrina Sangster.

TO MAKE THE STOCK SOLUTION

1. Grind indigo with pestle and mortar if necessary. (Sometimes it comes in resin form).

2. Stir into a paste with methylated spirits.

3. Stirring carefully, add the warm water, caustic soda and sodium dithionite in that order. Shake the chemicals in slowly to avoid lumps.

4. Leave to stand for at least one hour in a container with a tight-fitting lid. You can keep the stock for longer without any change in effectiveness, as long as the container is airtight.

TO USE THE STOCK SOLUTION

1. Use a large pot with a tight-fitting lid, at least 5 litres so there is room for the fibre to move about in the liquid.

2. Heat the water to 50°C.

3. Gradually add about half a cup of sodium dithionite to reduce the oxygen in the water. The lid has to be kept on as much as possible to prevent oxygen from getting in again.

4. Leave the pot to settle for a few minutes.

5. Tip the stock solution under the surface of the water, taking care to keep oxygen out as much as possible.

6. The dyebath should be clear yellow with occasional specks of blue.

7. Add a little more dithionite if the bath seems blue and not yellow.

8. Test the bath with a stick or stainless-steel spoon by dipping it into the liquid; it should come out yellow and turn blue in the manner of litmus paper.

9. Enter the clean, thoroughly wet fibre, leave for 10 minutes and pull out into the air for 10 minutes.

10. Repeat these dippings for a darker colour, keeping in mind that equal amounts of time spent in the dyebath and in contact with the air are what gives a strong, colourfast dye.

11. Rinse fibres thoroughly (you can do this in the rinse and spin cycle of your washing machine, as long as you rinse it through again before doing any laundry).

12. Hang to dry.

The same procedure can be followed with hanks which have been dyed with cochineal, madder or yellow dyes, taking care to soak them and squeeze out the excess moisture before putting them into the indigo vat. The previous dyes will interact with the indigo and produce shades of purple and green.

Taking it further

Choosing a loom

Once you have experimented with frame looms and have begun to build up a design portfolio, you may discover a growing interest in more complicated weave structures. This is the time to join a weavers' group or meet individually with other weavers so that you can experiment with frame looms that have systems for lifting the shed. You will also want to look at table looms, belt looms or other designs, and hopefully have an opportunity to weave a few yards on a big loom that is already set up, or to help with the setting-up process.

From this, you can get an idea of whether this is something you enjoy enough to invest in the equipment for future use. You can also assess how much space you have available to set up a loom, which might have to be a semi-permanent piece of furniture if you embark on a long-term project at home. Investigating in this way is well worth the time and effort if you can then make an informed choice. You may find there's a loom out there with your name on it and a built-in seat that fits you perfectly.

This certainly happened to me. After spending two years learning the basics from my friend Astrid and experimenting with borrowed equipment and community weaving sheds, helping friends to set up and learning all I could, I finally enrolled in a summer course at HV Skola in Stockholm. There, I experienced six weeks of strict basic training, which I have built on since, and came away with a glimmer of hope that I had completed several structural pieces and had a vague idea of how it all fitted together.

I decided to look for a four-shaft floor loom which would allow me to work with what I'd learned for the foreseeable future. The one requirement was that it must be portable, because I'd be leaving Stockholm the next year when I'd finished what I thought was my main achievement – my academic degree.

I placed an ad in the Stockholm daily paper and received several phone calls in reply. I narrowed it down to three. A friend with a van came with me to look at them. When we got to the third address I was a bit disheartened,

OPPOSITE PAGE *Silk rug weaving on a hand loom in China. Photo: Lee Prince/Shutterstock.*

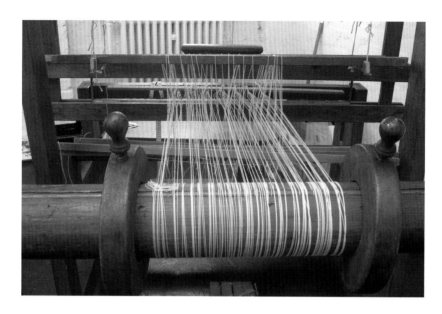

Swedish loom viewed from the back, showing the warp threads wound, spaced evenly and held in tension from the front of the loom.

because the first two had proved expensive and not so portable. On arrival, we were taken up to the attic storage area and there on the floor was a pile of very beautiful old wood, obviously hand carved in places, with one small tree trunk which turned out to be the back warp beam.

The wood had been there for 28 years because it had belonged to the mother of the seller, who was not a weaver herself. She wanted £10 for us to take the wood away; we were happy to oblige. When we got it home, it was a complete loom, portable and functioning in perfect balance after all those years. The back beam was a whole small tree trunk. I transported that loom to Arran and have used it for the past 35 years to weave and teach. The loom is in storage at the moment, ready for the next person whose destiny will be changed by a pile of beautifully crafted wood and whose bottom fits perfectly on the built-in seat.

Once you find a loom you like, it becomes an important part of your life. Learning to use it will be a creative journey of many years, so it's important to get the right loom to begin with. Sometimes it's a wonderful gift to inherit a loom from a friend or family member, or to be given one that is no longer in use. However, this can also be quite frustrating: I've seen students become disillusioned when things didn't go quite right with a loom they have taken over. As it's a very personal thing, this is not surprising. If you take up weaving because you feel obliged to use a particular loom, don't be surprised if it doesn't work smoothly for you. After all these years of weaving, I'll do anything to avoid using a table loom, though I can perfectly well keep my opinions to myself and show another person how to set one up and use it with great satisfaction.

If you're given a loom that doesn't work particularly well for you, you may want to weigh up the sentimental value and trade it for one that feels better.

If you feel you need to keep the one you've been given, consider trying out different ones available in a weaving group or course. Choose a loom that's going to make you happy – you'll be together for a long time if all goes well and your passion grows. For me the best thing about my loom was that it fitted my body perfectly.

The treadles were the right distance from the seat and I could reach easily to straighten out a thread or a heddle without straining any part of my body. This was important as I spent many hours weaving, bearing in mind the words of one young man who visited the studio. He was from Harris and had trained as a tweed weaver, but had to give it up because he couldn't make a living at weaving. Besides, he realised that the weavers who were older than him were the only workers who staggered when walking to the pub after a long working day.

COMBINING WEAVING WITH OTHER CRAFTS

Combining weaving with other crafts gives you a whole new area to experiment with once you feel confident about basic techniques. For example, embroidery stitches combine well with weaving to outline shapes or create a graphic line on a plain woven background. You can find a wealth of instructions for different embroidery stitches on the internet, see Further reading and information on page 103–5 for some suggestions.

Celtic Wedding (1987), by author. 50 x 50 cm. The background is a plain weave using hand-spun silk and alpaca on a cotton rug warp. The number of warp threads per inch and the relative thickness of warp and weft mean that the warp is covered. The figures are embroidered as the weaving progresses, using backstitch and French knots.

Weaving in the community – a memoir

Arran projects for inspiration

These projects were developed in the course of my work on the Isle of Arran, Scotland, but there is ample evidence of teachers and weavers worldwide who have successfully adapted the ideas to their own classroom situation and local environment to document and preserve their traditions.

INTRODUCING SPINNING

On one primary-school visit, I showed the children some grey Shetland fleece and demonstrated how to strengthen the fibres by twisting the fleece between their fingers and spinning a few inches of yarn. This was followed by a demonstration with an improvised spindle made from driftwood weighted with a rock from the beach. I tied the rock like a parcel to the driftwood with string to hold it firmly.

A few minutes later, one of the boys had turned his water bottle into a stable horizontal spindle on his desk, producing and winding an impressive few inches of yarn. One of the girls used a glue stick in one hand, fleece in the other, to achieve a similar result.

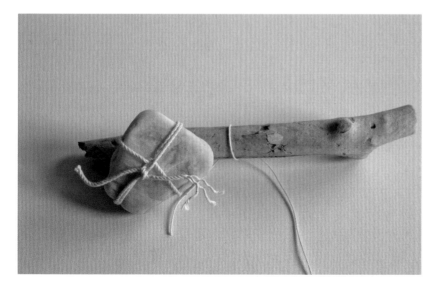

Spindle made from driftwood and stone.

OPPOSITE PAGE **Arran heritage tapestry**. *Photograph courtesy of the Arran Heritage Project.*

WEAVING

I left them at lunchtime prepared to carry on in the afternoon, getting the weaving sequence in the right order, managing their shuttles and making sure the edges weren't pulling in too tight.

Karen, their teacher, later wrote: 'The children … are all completely engrossed! It is really interesting to see that the children who have really taken to it aren't necessarily the same ones who show most ability in other art/craft techniques.'

The model for introducing weaving into curriculum work can be transferred effectively to an urban environment, as my past experience shows. One young teacher in a school in Kilmarnock who field-tested 'Connecting Threads' reported back that introducing weaving in her classroom work had opened up new possibilities in the Social Studies curriculum. The children could now focus on the history of Kilmarnock as a weaving town. Several of the class had found that they had weavers in their own family tree.

The skills can also be incorporated into many areas of the school curriculum to provide a focus for the wider study of culture, social studies and practical subjects like mathematics. In this way the craft is preserved but the context is contemporary, and we are ensuring that they are not lost entirely.

The introduction of weaving into the formal school curriculum happened very gradually over the years that I have been going into schools, introducing the skills and demonstrating techniques. From the beginning the sessions were very popular and it was clear from the children's silence and concentration that the crafts appealed to them and that they felt a sense of achievement in their skills and the finished pieces.

The weaving sessions in individual primary schools progressed to the point that in the spring term we brought Primary 7s together from different schools to the island high school once a week. This gave them an outing and an opportunity to meet pupils from other villages to work on developing skills. At this point the project was expanded into the home economics department for third and fourth year high-school pupils as part of their 'Fleece to Fabric' programme.

This segued nicely into the work of the art department in connection with the Arran Heritage Project, where for several years first-year pupils had been interviewing older members of the community, finding out more about the history of their villages. Weaving was demonstrated at the Arran Heritage Museum on the days when the pupils came to see traditional skills being practised and could try them out for themselves.

The Arran Heritage Tapestry was one result of collaboration between my studio, the art department and the heritage project.

THE ARRAN HERITAGE TAPESTRY

The curriculum work which began in the primary schools on the island gradually extended into Arran High School. Weaving skills were taught to third and fourth year pupils as part of the Arran heritage project, an inter-departmental programme at the school involving pupils from the first year onwards in research and interviews with the older residents of the island to record the island's cultural history.

Small frames were used to teach the basic techniques of tapestry weaving which would be required to produce the final pieces. Some inventive chickens, sheep and flowers appeared at this time, providing amusement and a steep learning curve. The yarns for this project were hand-spun and natural dyed, in keeping with traditional Arran recipes, providing a record of yet another aspect of the cultural history of the island.

The tapestry project developed in stages, centring around the ruins of three stone buildings and a row of cottages which had played an integral role in textile production on the island before industrialisation in the nineteenth century moved production to the mainland. Pupils from the art department photographed and sketched the ruins of the textile mills and the weavers' village. From their photos and sketches, drawings were produced of how the buildings might have looked when they were in operation. These drawings were then simplified into cartoons which were placed behind the tapestry looms to guide the weavers in producing the final picture. Four panels were produced, and were sewn together to create the finished work.

CHILDREN'S SUMMER WEAVING WORKSHOPS

In addition to working in schools on Arran, for many years I held weaving workshops on the island for children during the summer. At one point, the venue was an old military tent in a field until we built a more sophisticated studio. Sometimes we had more than twenty children in an afternoon, but we never had disciplinary problems. They were too absorbed in their work and often disappointed when their parents came to collect them.

We threaded up the looms ahead of the workshops so that all the time could be spent weaving. We then taught basic weaving and simple interlocking, and progressed to more complicated designs on an individual basis, depending on the abilities of the child. Sometimes an entire family came to try out the weaving. They often told me afterwards that they had

Weaving by a young football supporter.

One basket of yarns, one family,
five distinct weavings.

not only learned new skills but had something new to discuss over dinner at the end of the day and a sense of togetherness not always found on holiday.

One of the joys of the summer weaving workshops was meeting a child in the village the next day, proudly carrying and using their new purse. I still meet twenty-year-olds who tell me that they have their weavings hanging on their bedroom wall along with the current pop band posters.

STUDENT APPRENTICESHIPS

My studio at Silverbirch on Arran hosted a number of apprentices in the 1970s and 1980s when students from colleges in the UK and the USA came as part of their art, textile or carpet design courses. They were sent to the studio to work for a few weeks in a rural island environment, helping with the production of yarn which was hand-spun and natural dyed, usually from local sheep. Depending on which course they were in at college, they also worked on independent design and weave projects to develop their knowledge and skill of hand production in the textile crafts.

The project records from the studio in those years not only show how the students' confidence in their design and exhibition skills grew, they also provide a rich archive of ideas and techniques as a resource for other weavers. The apprentices' work usually formed an important part of their degree show.

Shelley's screen

One apprentice's project was an old wooden room screen with four hinged panels which was turned into a loom. Along the top and bottom of each panel, the nails which had formerly held the fabric in place were still intact and in good enough condition to hold the warp threads. The screen was warped up with 2-ply chunky hand-spun yarn in natural shades over the four separate panels, leaving the hinges free.

The tree design illustrated began with a simple diagonal weave in the bottom-right corner and a narrow 'branch' higher up. The second panel continued the theme of three branches reaching across, two ending at the top of the third panel, the third carrying across the last panel. In the third and fourth panels, leaves were introduced randomly to complete the design and the screen was ready for use again.

The screen illustrates a weaving technique where only the design part of the piece is actually woven, in this case the leaves and tree trunks. The rest of the warp is left transparent, creating a light and airy effect in the finished work.

Shelley's screen, (c. 1980), handspun wool. 2.44 m high.

This technique must be woven either on a frame that will become part of the finished piece (as with the screen described above), or on a sturdy 'frame' of yarn stretched firmly across the top and bottom and along the two sides, so that the weave doesn't collapse when you cut it off the loom.

Adult education and inter-generational work

In the early 1990s my own life changed and in the course of re-evaluating what I wanted to do – which included the possibility of giving up textiles altogether and returning to academic studies, I was catapulted firmly back to the island by the organisers of a Women's Development course I attended at the University of Strathclyde in Glasgow. They asked me to set up a traditional textile course for women over 50, to teach spinning and weaving to an age group where these skills had been lost, even though crafts like knitting and embroidery still featured in their lives. The class ran for several years, one result of which was production of the Arran Tapestry for Beijing (see following page).

As I was still working with primary-school pupils and the over-50s group was gaining in proficiency, it was a natural development that they become tutors for the Primary 7s and their teachers. The pupils and teachers gained from the experience of the older members of the community, not only in acquiring textile skills. As a result of these years of building up communication and teaching skills between the generations, the programme was awarded significant funding from the National Lottery and the Scottish Arts Council to develop the work and share it through production of a learning pack, CD Rom and video for teachers who wanted to integrate the traditions into classroom and curriculum planning.

The first island project, Project Orchil, was named after the purple colour extracted by ancient dyers from shellfish, to be used only for royal robes. Its three-year courses were aimed at adults, who would then be proficient in teaching the traditional skills as part of classroom work. Other courses, such as business development, building personal confidence and computer skills, were aimed at supplementing textile knowledge. This put weaving into the context of a rural island economy, creating the possibility of part-time self-employment in the tourism market. We were visited by other groups from Europe through European Union exchanges, and realised that the concept of setting up micro-businesses was gaining momentum with support from the EU, especially in rural areas.

Project Orchil contributed to the development of study programmes which are still in evidence today as part of initiatives in Europe and in developing countries to promote rural economies and address depopulation in communities where textile skills formerly provided vital back-up to farming and fishing. There is a long way to go before these programmes become a recognised strand of formal learning, but there is also a heartening recognition worldwide that we should not let these skills die out.

The second major programme which developed on the island was Project Charlotte, named after the famous spider who saved the pig in E.B. White's story Charlotte's Web. The tutors who had trained in Project Orchil visited the island's primary schools, teaching textile skills to fit in with the individual topics that each school was exploring as part of curriculum work. One example was the construction of a stone-weight loom based on those used by the Vikings who inhabited the island for four hundred years from the fifth century. A programme based on weaving skills lends itself well to classroom planning for this topic, and covered much more than the skills themselves.

WOMEN WEAVING THE WORLD TOGETHER – BEIJING, 1995

Weaving a large tapestry is an excellent way to bring people together to learn new skills and share knowledge. In 1995 this idea was adopted internationally with 'Women Weaving the World Together', a project which began in Cambodia with women producing 1 x 1 metre weavings for the United Nations Conference on Women in Beijing. The individual pieces were then taken to China and sewn together into a 2 kilometre strip which was displayed for the cameras on the Great Wall of China, despite heavy rain and a strong police presence.

Our group was contacted by the UK delegation and asked to participate in producing a panel for the tapestry. The contribution from Arran was a 'map' of the island, based on the Geological Survey map. Each participant wove an area that represented some special part of the island in her life. She chose natural fibres and dyes to resonate with her own experience and memory.

Sewing the tapestry together in Beijing.

Arran *tapestry for Beijing.*

The weaving brief was simple: don't leave any holes in the weave when you link to the next person's contribution. The design was random, but it worked. The final piece was not only an icon of the island, but a sampler of weaving and a record of personal experience from each woman involved.

Epilogue

Writing this book has been a journey back through the past 40 years. Deciding what to include and how to explain the intricacies of weaving without being physically present as a teacher has been a great experience and challenge for me.

I'm aware that my life is not unlike the weavings in this book, bringing together ideas and creativity to form a whole picture. Even at that, I'm sure the work is not finished and I know that the book will provide inspiration and motivation for me and for you to keep the craft alive, preserving but not smothering it.

Further reading and information

As a beginner it isn't necessary to invest in a large and costly library. The books and CDs recommended here are reprints of the books that I bought for my library in the 1970s and 1980s. Their content is still relevant today.

My 'library' consists mainly of magazine articles, inspirational photos and postcards of weavings which students and friends have sent over the years. More recently, I have added a list of websites where I can find the information that I need to develop my work or to look back at ideas that I have used in the past.

WEAVING

Znamierowski, Nell, *Step by Step Weaving* (Golden Press, 1967)

Black, Mary, *New Key to Weaving* (Macmillan Publishing Company, 1978)

SPINNING

Davenport, Elsie, *Your Handspinning* (Select Books, 1978)

Casey, Maggie, *Start Spinning: Everything You Need to Know to Make Great Yarn* (Interweave Press, 2008)

Mackenzie McCuin, Judith, *The Intentional Spinner: A Holistic Approach to Spinning Yarn* (Interweave Press, 2010)

NATURAL DYEING

Dean, Jenny, *The Craft of Natural Dyeing: Glowing Colours from the Plant World* (Search Press, 1998)

Lambert, Eva and Tracey Kendall, *The Complete Guide to Natural Dyeing* (Search Press, 2010)

EMBROIDERY

The Embroiderers' Guild www.embroiderersguild.com

Needle 'n Thread www.needlenthread.com

GLOBAL ECONOMY IN THE TWENTY-FIRST CENTURY

Sirolli, Ernesto, *Ripples from the Zambezi: Passion, Entrepreneurship, and the Rebirth of Local Economies* (Sirolli Institute, 1999)

Novogratz, Jacqueline, *The Blue Sweater* (Rodale Press 2009)

COMMUNITY WEAVING PROJECTS

Village projects in Lesotho, www.setsotodesign.com

Trade projects worldwide, www.traidcraft.co.uk

TEACHING RESOURCES

Heal, Gillian, *Grandpa Bear's Fantastic Scarf* (Beyond Words Publishing, 1996)

Arran Textiles Multimedia Presentation, Connecting Threads (2000) available from SCRAN (Scottish Cultural Resource Access Network), www.scran.ac.uk

INSPIRATION AND DESIGN

Ramses Wissa Wassef Art Centre, Egypt. www.wissa-wassef-arts.com

Since 1952, two generations of weavers have developed in the Art Centre that Ramses Wissa Wassef established with his wife Sophie at Harrania, near Giza. Nine of the original group of children who began working around the age of twelve, many of them now grandparents, are still weaving under the guidance of Sophie Wissa Wassef. A second generation of weavers, guided by the Wissa Wassefs' daughters Suzanne and Yoanna, continue to produce wool and cotton tapestries that are remarkable and unique works of art.

Collingwood, Peter, *Textile and Weaving Structures* (Batsford, 1987)

WEAVING COURSES

If you want to learn more about cloth- and/or tapestry-weaving, the internet is a good source of information about courses (both informal and degree level), museums and conservation work. Spinning and weaving guilds near you are an excellent source of practical advice and tuition.

Below are listed some contemporary tapestry studios that I know first hand or which have been recommended to me by students and colleagues, where techniques are taught to a high standard and apprenticeships are available to learn the craft professionally.

UK

Dovecot, Edinburgh, Scotland
www.dovecotstudios.com

Handweavers Studio and Gallery, London, England
www.handweavers.co.uk

The Stirling Tapestries, Stirling Castle, Scotland
www.stirlingcastle.gov.uk

West Dean, West Sussex, England
www.org.uk

USA

Pacific Textile Arts, Fort Bragg, California
www.pacifictextilearts.org

Vavstuga Weaving School, Massachusetts
www.vavstuga.com

SWEDEN

HV Skola, Stockholm, Sweden
www.hvskola.se

Suppliers

To keep up to date with general weaving information, see my website, Rainbow Textiles, www.lynngrayross.co.uk.

Knitting and yarn shops are a good source of weaving yarns. Charity shops are a good source of recycled yarn.

Ravelry has information on yarn suppliers and courses, www.ravelry.com

Handweavers Studio and Gallery, London, www.handweavers.co.uk

Vavstuga Weaving School, Massachusetts, USA (yarn and equipment), www.vavstuga.com

Scottish Fibres (yarn and equipment), www.scottishfibres.co.uk

Fibrecraft (yarn, equipment, books, etc.), www.fibrecrafts.com

Earthues (natural dyes and other supplies, courses with Michele Wipplinger), www.earthues.com

Australian Tapestry Workshop, Melbourne, Victoria (Tapestry Commission and Production) www.austapestry.com.au

WARP (Weave A Real Peace) is a networking organisation of weavers, academics, and interested supporters who value the importance of textiles to communities around the world, www.weavearealpeace.org

Glossary

Aran wool – traditionally used for Irish knitting, this is an ideal thickness for weaving on the small frame loom.

cloth – the finished product of weaving, used for clothing or household textiles.

drafts – written patterns which tell the weaver how to thread up a loom to produce the desired cloth design.

hank – wool wound off the spinning wheel or machine, usually measurable in lengths to help calculate amounts needed for weaving a specific project.

heddle – a metal or string 'eye' through which warp yarns are threaded to keep them separate during weaving. The order in which the heddles are threaded helps to form the finished pattern.

Jacquard – a system of punched cards invented in 1801, connected to the loom to facilitate the weaving of damask and other complicated patterns.

loom – a piece of equipment used to hold one set of threads in tension so that a second set of threads can be passed over and under in sequence to produce cloth.

niddy-noddy – a tool used to make skeins from yarn. Traditionally made of wood, it consists of a central bar, with crossbars at either end, offset from each other by 90°. The most common length of a niddy-noddy skein is two yards around, enabling the weaver to measure the total yardage of the skein.

ply – a strand of fibre produced in spinning, twisted either clockwise or anti-clockwise. Usually combined with more strands to form a thicker yarn known for example as 2-ply or 3-ply.

shaft – denotes the number of sheds possible in the warp threads on a loom. On a frame loom there are two possible sheds where one set of threads is lifted and the other remains in place.

shed – the opening created when one set of warp threads is lifted away from the others.

shuttle – a piece of equipment round which yarn is wound to carry it through the shed.

skeiner – one device used to wind spun yarn into measurable lengths.

spindle – 1) a wooden spike traditionally used for spinning fibres into thread. It is usually weighted at the bottom (sometimes called a drop spindle), most commonly by a circular or spherical object called a whorl, and may also have a hook, groove or notch, though spindles without these are also common. Spindle whorls have been found in archaeological digs around the world. 2) part of a spinning wheel or of an industrial spinning machine.

spinning – the process of twisting fibre into yarn, either by hand or industrially.

twist – the direction of spinning: clockwise or anti-clockwise, important in determining the finished design of yarn and cloth.

warp – the threads which are in tension on a loom to form the basis of weaving.

weft – the threads which go under and over the warp during weaving, to form the pattern of the finished cloth.

yarn – fibre strengthened by twist in the spinning process, often with two or more strands or plies twisted together to form a thicker, stronger fibre.

Index